WEEKEND PLEASU

Canadian Living's™ best

BY

Elizabeth Baird

AND

The Food Writers of Canadian Living Magazine
and The Canadian Living Test Kitchen

A MADISON PRESS BOOK

PRODUCED FOR

BALLANTINE BOOKS AND CANADIAN LIVING™

Ballantine Books
A Division of
Random House of
Canada Limited
1265 Aerowood Drive
Mississauga, Ontario
Canada
L4W 1B9

Canadian Living
Telemedia
Communications Inc.
25 Sheppard Avenue West
Suite 100
North York, Ontario
Canada
M2N 6S7

Canadian Cataloguing in Publication Data

Weekend pleasures

(Canadian living's best)
Includes index.
ISBN 0-345-39806-8

1. Cookery, Canadian.
I. Title.   II. Series.

TX715.6.B35 1996   641.5971   C96-930868-X

™Canadian Living is a trademark owned by
Telemedia Communications Inc. and licensed by The Madison Press Limited.
All trademark rights, registered and unregistered, are reserved worldwide.

EDITORIAL DIRECTOR: Hugh Brewster
SUPERVISING EDITOR: Wanda Nowakowska
PROJECT EDITOR: Beverley Sotolov
EDITORIAL ASSISTANCE: Beverley Renahan
PRODUCTION DIRECTOR: Susan Barrable
PRODUCTION COORDINATOR: Donna Chong
BOOK DESIGN AND LAYOUT: Gordon Sibley Design Inc.
COLOR SEPARATION: Colour Technologies
PRINTING AND BINDING: St. Joseph Printing Limited

CANADIAN LIVING ADVISORY BOARD: Elizabeth Baird, Bonnie Baker Cowan,
Anna Hobbs, Caren King

CANADIAN LIVING'S™ BEST WEEKEND PLEASURES
was produced by Madison Press Books,
which is under the direction of Albert E. Cummings

Madison Press Books
40 Madison Avenue
Toronto, Ontario, Canada
M5R 2S1

Printed in Canada

Contents

Introduction

It's the weekend at last! Now you have time to cook and to share special moments with family and friends. Sure there are chores to do and obligations to fulfill, but these two days are often the time when the traditions of hospitality can be renewed — from a birthday party for your best friend to an impromptu nibbles-and-drinks gathering after the game. And nothing tops a weekend dinner party. Whether the guest list is old friends or a "let's introduce so-and-so to so-and-so" occasion, it's a chance to dress up, sit down together over a creative and pleasant repast and enjoy one another's company. No longer are dinner parties show-off events. The menus that dazzle these days are delicious, simple to put together and affordable.

The weekend can also provide opportunities for sharing the pleasures of cooking with young children and passing on your skills to a new generation of curious cooks. The cookies may take longer to shape, the cake may look a little lopsided, but the satisfaction children discover in creating food is plenty of reward. For food lovers and hobby cooks, the weekend is the perfect time to get up early for the market, head out to the country for just-picked apples or explore ethnic grocery stores. Then it's back to the kitchen to try something novel and intriguing or to master baking bread or creating the ultimate phyllo wrap.

I believe you'll find everything you need in *Weekend Pleasures* to make your weekends more fun, relaxing and delicious. Please join me as we fill our homes with the aromas of a welcoming kitchen and share the delectable results at the table. *Bon appétit!*

Elizabeth Baird

Halibut Package with Dill Pesto
(recipe, p. 54)

Entertaining in Style

When it's time to pull out all the stops for a dazzling dinner party, family birthday or anniversary celebration, a delectable menu from this chapter provides all the inspiration you need. For dessert finales, see Sweet Endings (last chapter).

MENU

NO-PANIC DINNER PARTY

Easy, make-ahead — and impressive.
What more could you ask for in an entertaining menu?

MAKE-AHEAD SEAFOOD SALAD
MAPLE ORANGE CORNISH HENS
ZUCCHINI RIBBONS
SQUASH CRESCENTS
RICE AND SWEET PEPPER PILAF

Maple Orange Cornish Hens

Cornish hens are still one of the most popular choices for a great dinner. If you prefer, cook the birds whole, as in the photo, easing orange rind in between skin and breast, then tying the legs together and roasting in 375°F (190°C) oven for 1 hour. Use kitchen shears to cut the hens into halves to serve.

Per serving: about
- 385 calories
- 19 g fat
- good source of iron
- 38 g protein
- 13 g carbohydrate

1/3 cup	maple syrup or packed brown sugar	75 mL
1/3 cup	orange juice	75 mL
2 tbsp	white wine (optional)	25 mL
2 tsp	chopped dried rosemary	10 mL
3	Cornish hens (about 1-1/4 lb/625 g each)	3
1 tbsp	finely grated orange rind	15 mL
Pinch	each salt and pepper	Pinch
	Fresh rosemary sprigs and orange slices	

● In small saucepan, whisk together maple syrup, orange juice, wine (if using) and rosemary. Bring to boil; boil for 3 to 5 minutes or until glaze is slightly thickened. Let cool slightly.

● Meanwhile, cut wing tips from hens. Using kitchen shears or sharp knife, cut along each side of backbone; discard backbone. Cut through breastbone to separate into halves. Trim off excess fat and skin. Gently loosen skin from each half of hens, leaving skin attached at back side. Starting at breast, ease in orange rind over flesh under skin.

● Place hens, skin side up, on foil-lined baking sheet. Sprinkle with salt and pepper; brush with one-third of the glaze. Roast in 375°F (190°C) oven, brushing with glaze twice, for 45 minutes or until browned and juices run clear when hen is pierced.

● Arrange hens on serving platter; garnish with rosemary and orange slices. Makes 6 servings.

Zucchini Ribbons

The secret to tasty zucchini is quick cooking and a good dollop of zesty ingredients such as garlic, coriander seeds and wine vinegar.

Per serving: about
- 50 calories
- 1 g protein
- 2 g fat
- 6 g carbohydrate

2	large zucchini (1-1/2 lb/750 g total)	2
1 tbsp	olive oil	15 mL
1	onion, chopped	1
2 tsp	white wine vinegar or cider vinegar	10 mL
2	cloves garlic, minced	2
1/2 tsp	salt	2 mL
1/4 tsp	crushed coriander seeds	1 mL
1/4 tsp	pepper	1 mL

● With vegetable peeler, cut zucchini lengthwise into thin strips; place in sieve. *(Zucchini can be prepared to this point, covered and set aside to drain for up to 8 hours.)* Blot up any liquid on strips.

● In large skillet, heat oil over medium-high heat; cook onion, vinegar, garlic, salt, coriander seeds and pepper, stirring, for 3 to 5 minutes or until softened. Stir in zucchini just until heated through, about 2 minutes. Serve immediately. Makes 6 servings.

Squash Crescents

An eye-catching shape and vivid color make acorn squash appealing for a dinner party.

Per serving: about
- 100 calories
- 2 g protein
- 2 g fat
- 21 g carbohydrate
- high source of fiber

1	large acorn squash	1
1 tbsp	butter	15 mL
1/4 tsp	curry powder	1 mL
1/4 tsp	salt	1 mL
1 tbsp	apple juice	15 mL

● With sharp knife, cut squash in half lengthwise; scoop out seeds and fibers. Place cut side down; cut crosswise into 1/2-inch (1 cm) thick crescents. Arrange in single layer in 13- x 9-inch (3 L) baking dish.

● In small saucepan, melt together butter, curry powder and salt over medium heat until bubbling; brush over squash. Cover and bake in 375°F (190°C) oven for about 20 minutes or just until tender. *(Squash can be prepared to this point, covered and set aside for up to 8 hours.)*

● Sprinkle squash with apple juice, turning to coat. Bake, uncovered, for about 5 minutes or until tender and glazed. Makes 6 servings.

Rice and Sweet Pepper Pilaf

Wild rice always adds a touch of glamour to a menu. Combine a small quantity with long-grain white rice and it's not an extravagance. Buying wild rice in bulk is often better value than opting for packaged or bagged.

Per serving: about
- 200 calories
- 6 g protein
- 3 g fat
- 31 g carbohydrate

1 tbsp	butter	15 mL
2	cloves garlic, minced	2
1	onion, chopped	1
1/2 tsp	dried thyme	2 mL
1/4 tsp	pepper	1 mL
1-1/2 cups	chicken or vegetable stock	375 mL
1 tbsp	white wine vinegar	15 mL
1/2 cup	wild rice, rinsed	125 mL
1 cup	long-grain rice	250 mL
Half	sweet red or yellow pepper, diced	Half
1/2 tsp	salt	2 mL

● In large saucepan, melt butter over medium heat; cook garlic, onion, thyme and pepper, stirring occasionally, until softened, about 5 minutes.

● Add stock, 1-1/4 cups (300 mL) water and vinegar; bring to boil. Add wild rice and return to boil; reduce heat, cover and simmer for 35 minutes.

● Stir in long-grain rice; cover and simmer for about 30 minutes or until rice is tender and liquid is absorbed. With fork, stir in red pepper and salt; cover and let stand for 5 minutes. Makes 6 servings.

Make-Ahead Seafood Salad ▲

1	small onion, chopped	1
1	bay leaf	1
12 oz	raw medium shrimp	375 g
1	head Boston lettuce	1
Half	sweet red pepper	Half
	DRESSING	
2 tbsp	light mayonnaise	25 mL
1 tbsp	lime or lemon juice	15 mL
Dash	hot pepper sauce	Dash
1/2 cup	buttermilk	125 mL
1/4 cup	chopped chives or green onions	50 mL
1 tbsp	chopped fresh coriander or dill	15 mL
Pinch	salt	Pinch

● In saucepan, bring 4 cups (1 L) water, onion and bay leaf to boil; reduce heat and simmer for 5 minutes. Add shrimp; simmer for 2 to 4 minutes or until pink. Drain, peel and devein shrimp. Cover and refrigerate until chilled or for up to 4 hours.

● Meanwhile, separate lettuce into leaves; wash, dry and wrap in towels. *(Wrapped lettuce can be refrigerated in plastic bag for up to 1 day.)* Dice red pepper. *(Red pepper can be refrigerated in airtight container for up to 8 hours.)*

● DRESSING: In small bowl, whisk together mayonnaise, lime juice and hot pepper sauce; whisk in buttermilk, chives, coriander and salt until combined. *(Dressing can be covered and refrigerated for up to 8 hours.)*

● Arrange 2 or 3 lettuce leaves attractively in individual salad bowls. Sprinkle with about three-quarters of the red pepper. Mound shrimp on top. *(Salad can be prepared to this point, covered and refrigerated for up to 1 hour.)* Drizzle with dressing; sprinkle with remaining red pepper. Makes 6 servings.

T*his appetizer salad can be made ahead and assembled just before guests arrive. The servings can wait, lightly covered, on plates in the refrigerator. Add a few cherry tomatoes or tomatoes cut in wedges, if desired, and drizzle on the dressing just before carrying the salads to the table.*

Per serving: about
- 80 calories
- 3 g fat
- 10 g protein
- 3 g carbohydrate

BUFFET FOR TWELVE

*If you like the idea of not having to be in the kitchen when company comes, you'll love this
help-yourself menu starring a boneless double breast of turkey.*

ROASTED ROLLED TURKEY BREAST
SWEET POTATO AND APPLE CASSEROLE
CRANBERRY AND PINEAPPLE CHUTNEY
SAGE GARLIC BREAD
GREEN BEAN AND RED PEPPER SALAD

Roasted Rolled Turkey Breast

1	boneless rolled turkey breast (about 4 lb/2 kg)	1
1/3 cup	lemon juice	75 mL
1/4 cup	sweet prepared mustard	50 mL
1/4 cup	olive oil	50 mL
2 tbsp	balsamic or red wine vinegar	25 mL
2 tsp	chopped fresh rosemary (or 2 tsp/10 mL dried)	10 mL
1 tsp	dried thyme	5 mL
2	cloves garlic, minced	2
1/4 cup	toasted chopped pecans (optional)	50 mL

● Place turkey breast in large glass baking dish. Combine lemon juice, mustard, all but 1 tbsp (15 mL) of the oil, vinegar, rosemary, thyme and garlic. Pour over turkey, turning to coat. Cover and refrigerate for 24 hours, turning occasionally.

● Brush marinade from turkey, reserving marinade. In large skillet, heat remaining oil over medium-high heat; brown turkey breast on both sides, about 7 minutes.

● Place on greased rack in roasting pan; roast in 325°F (160°C) oven, basting every 30 minutes with marinade and pan drippings, for about 2 hours or until meat thermometer registers 170°F (77°C).

● Transfer to cutting board and tent with foil; let stand for 20 minutes before slicing thinly. Serve garnished with pecans (if using). Makes 12 servings.

Mustard creates a delicious glaze for this rolled double turkey breast. Avoid bright-yellow mustards and instead choose a Russian- or Scandinavian-style sweet prepared mustard such as "Honeycup."

Per serving: about
- 220 calories
- 7 g fat
- 35 g protein
- 3 g carbohydrate

Sweet Potato and Apple Casserole

4 lb	large sweet potatoes (about 8)	2 kg
5	apples, peeled and thinly sliced	5
1 cup	chicken stock	250 mL
2 tbsp	butter	25 mL
1 tbsp	lemon juice	15 mL
1-1/2 tsp	each salt and pepper	7 mL
	TOPPING	
2 cups	fresh bread crumbs	500 mL
1/4 cup	butter, melted	50 mL

● Peel and cut sweet potatoes into large chunks. In large pot of boiling water, cook sweet potatoes, covered, for 10 to 15 minutes or just until tender. Drain and return to pot.

● Meanwhile, in large skillet, combine apples and 1/4 cup (50 mL) of the stock; cook, covered, over medium heat for 5 to 10 minutes or just until tender. Add to sweet potatoes along with remaining stock, butter, lemon juice, salt and pepper; mash lightly. Transfer to food processor, in batches, and purée until smooth. *(Purée can be prepared to this point and refrigerated in airtight container for up to 2 days, or frozen for up to 1 week; thaw in refrigerator for 36 hours.)*

● In saucepan, cook sweet potato mixture over medium heat, stirring occasionally, for about 10 minutes or until heated through. Spoon into greased 13- x 9-inch (3 L) baking dish.

● TOPPING: Toss bread crumbs with butter; spread evenly over purée. Broil for 1 to 2 minutes or until golden brown and crispy. Makes 12 servings.

Puréed vegetables are easy to reheat and serve buffet-style, making them good choices when entertaining a crowd.

Per serving: about
- 265 calories
- 7 g fat
- high source of fiber
- 4 g protein
- 49 g carbohydrate

TIP: Use your microwave on Defrost or Low to speed up thawing vegetable purées, and on Medium to reheat.

Cranberry and Pineapple Chutney

When fresh pineapple is available, chop some up for this lovely red chutney. Or use canned, either crushed or chunks.

Per tbsp (15 mL): about
- 25 calories
- 0 g fat
- trace of protein
- 6 g carbohydrate

4 cups	fresh or frozen cranberries	1 L
1 cup	golden raisins	250 mL
3/4 cup	granulated sugar	175 mL
3/4 cup	crushed or chopped fresh pineapple	175 mL
1/2 cup	finely chopped celery	125 mL
1/2 cup	pineapple juice	125 mL
3 tbsp	white vinegar	50 mL
1 tsp	finely chopped gingerroot	5 mL
1/2 tsp	cinnamon	2 mL

● In saucepan, combine cranberries, raisins, sugar, pineapple, celery, pineapple juice, vinegar, ginger and cinnamon; bring to boil.

● Reduce heat to medium; cook, stirring often, for 15 to 20 minutes or until thickened and most of the liquid is absorbed. Let cool to room temperature. *(Chutney can be refrigerated in airtight container for up to 2 weeks.)* Makes 4 cups (1 L).

Sage Garlic Bread

The irresistible flavor of sage in this crisp bread is more vibrant if you make the bread a day ahead.

Per serving: about
- 240 calories
- 12 g fat
- 5 g protein
- 28 g carbohydrate

2/3 cup	butter, softened	150 mL
1 tbsp	finely chopped chives or green onion	15 mL
1 tbsp	finely chopped fresh parsley	15 mL
1 tbsp	dried sage (or 3 tbsp/50 mL chopped fresh)	15 mL
2	cloves garlic, minced	2
1/2 tsp	pepper	2 mL
2	thin 20-inch (50 cm) long baguettes	2

● In bowl, combine butter, chives, parsley, sage, garlic and pepper. Cut baguettes diagonally into 1-inch (2.5 cm) thick slices, cutting almost through to bottom.

● Spread butter mixture on both sides of each slice. Place each baguette on large piece of foil; wrap tightly to enclose bread. *(Bread can be prepared to this point and refrigerated for up to 24 hours.)*

● Bake in 325°F (160°C) oven for 30 to 40 minutes or until warmed through. Unwrap and broil for 2 minutes or until crisp. Makes 12 servings.

Green Bean and Red Pepper Salad

When making this colorful salad ahead, keep the dressing and green beans separate and toss them together just before serving.

Per serving: about
- 125 calories
- 9 g fat
- 2 g protein
- 9 g carbohydrate

2-1/2 lb	green beans	1.25 kg	Pinch	granulated sugar	Pinch
1 cup	thinly sliced red onion	250 mL	1/2 cup	olive oil	125 mL
2	sweet red peppers, julienned	2			
	DRESSING				
1/4 cup	lemon juice or red wine vinegar	50 mL			
1 tbsp	chopped fresh parsley	15 mL			
1 tbsp	Dijon mustard	15 mL			
3/4 tsp	salt	4 mL			
1/2 tsp	pepper	2 mL			
1	clove garlic, minced	1			

● In steamer or large pot of boiling salted water, cook green beans for 2 to 4 minutes or just until tender-crisp. Drain and cool under cold running water; drain well and place in large bowl. Add onion and red peppers.

● DRESSING: In small bowl, whisk together lemon juice, parsley, mustard, salt, pepper, garlic and sugar; gradually whisk in oil. Pour over salad and toss to coat well. Makes 12 servings.

WELCOME TO OUR OPEN HOUSE!

*Entertaining a crowd for nibbles and drinks is smooth sailing any time
of the year if the finger food is ready and waiting. Round out the welcome with coffee and tea,
plus mini pieces of wickedly rich dessert squares.*

FROSTY FRUIT PUNCH
STUFFED BAGUETTE SANDWICHES
MUSHROOM SQUARES
CALICO MUSSELS

Frosty Fruit Punch

A *block of commercial ice or an ice ring made from distilled water is better than ice cubes for keeping chilled punch refreshingly cold. The large chunk of ice melts more slowly than cubes, diluting the punch less.*

Per serving: about
- 100 calories
- trace of fat
- 1 g protein
- 25 g carbohydrate

1/2 cup	lemon juice	125 mL
1/4 cup	granulated sugar	50 mL
4 cups	grapefruit juice	1 L
4 cups	white grape juice	1 L
2 cups	orange juice	500 mL
2	oranges (unpeeled), sliced	2
1	lemon, sliced	1
	Ice block	
2	bottles (750 mL each) nonalcoholic sparkling apple cider or fruit juice	2
1/2 cup	vodka (optional)	125 mL

● In saucepan, stir lemon juice with sugar over medium heat until dissolved. Let cool.

● In very large bowl or pot, stir together lemon juice mixture, grapefruit juice, grape juice, orange juice, oranges and lemon. Pour into pitchers; cover and refrigerate until chilled. *(Punch can be prepared to this point and refrigerated for up to 24 hours.)*

● To serve, place ice block in punch bowl. Pour in fruit mixture; stir in apple cider, and vodka (if using). Makes twenty-five 3/4-cup (175 mL) servings.

Stuffed Baguette Sandwiches

P*arty sandwiches are easy to hold and always a hit at any gathering. Stuffing baguettes with two fillings — one based on a favorite egg salad, the other more Mediterranean in inspiration — adds an innovative, sure-to-please twist.*

Per hors d'oeuvre (Egg Salad Filling): about
- 40 calories
- 2 g fat
- 2 g protein
- 4 g carbohydrate

Per hors d'oeuvre (Mediterranean Filling): about
- 40 calories
- 2 g fat
- 2 g protein
- 4 g carbohydrate

2	thin 20-inch (50 cm) long baguettes	2
	EGG SALAD FILLING	
6	hard-cooked eggs	6
2 cups	watercress, trimmed and chopped	500 mL
1/4 cup	minced red onion	50 mL
2 tbsp	cream cheese, softened	25 mL
2 tbsp	light mayonnaise	25 mL
1 tbsp	Dijon mustard	15 mL
1/4 tsp	each salt and pepper	1 mL
1/4 tsp	curry powder (optional)	1 mL
Pinch	cayenne pepper	Pinch
	MEDITERRANEAN FILLING	
1	jar (6 oz/170 mL) marinated artichoke hearts	1
1/4 cup	minced black olives	50 mL
1	small clove garlic, minced	1
1	pkg (250 g) light cream cheese, softened	1
1	jar (212 g) roasted red peppers, drained and patted dry	1

● Cut 1 of the baguettes in half crosswise; cut off ends. Using wooden spoon, push out bread from inside to hollow out each half, leaving 1/2-inch (1 cm) thick walls.

● EGG SALAD FILLING: In bowl, mince eggs; stir in watercress, onion, cream cheese, mayonnaise, mustard, salt, pepper, curry powder (if using) and cayenne. Holding each half of cut baguette on end, pack filling into bread shells with wooden spoon.

● Cut off top third of remaining baguette lengthwise; hollow out each piece, leaving 1/2-inch (1 cm) thick walls.

● MEDITERRANEAN FILLING: Reserving 2 tsp (10 mL) of the marinade, drain artichoke hearts and chop finely; set aside. In bowl, stir together olives, reserved artichoke marinade and garlic; spread over inside of bread shells. Spread with cream cheese. Arrange peppers and artichoke hearts over bottom shell; fit top shell over filling.

● Wrap each filled loaf tightly in foil; refrigerate for at least 4 hours or for up to 24 hours. To serve, cut each with serrated knife into 1/2-inch (1 cm) thick slices. Makes about 72 hors d'oeuvres.

Mushroom Squares

1/4 cup	butter	50 mL
1	onion, chopped	1
4	cloves garlic, minced	4
6-1/2 cups	sliced fresh exotic mushrooms (12 oz/375 g)	1.625 L
6 cups	sliced fresh mushrooms (1 lb/500 g)	1.5 L
1/2 cup	port or beef stock	125 mL
1/4 cup	chopped fresh parsley	50 mL
1/4 cup	cream cheese, softened	50 mL
4 tsp	lemon juice	20 mL
1 tsp	Worcestershire sauce	5 mL
Pinch	each salt and pepper	Pinch
2	eggs	2
1	pkg (411 g) thawed, puff pastry	1
1 tsp	(approx) milk or cream	5 mL
3 tbsp	dry bread crumbs	45 mL

● In skillet, melt butter over medium heat; cook onion and garlic for 2 minutes. Add exotic and regular mushrooms; cook for 2 minutes. Add port; reduce heat and simmer for 30 minutes or until liquid is almost evaporated. Stir in parsley, cheese, lemon juice, Worcestershire, salt and pepper until cheese is melted; let cool.

● Separate 1 of the eggs; set yolk aside for glaze. Whisk together egg white and remaining egg; blend into mushroom mixture.

● Roll half the pastry to fit 17- x 11-inch (45 x 29 cm) rimless baking sheet. Beat reserved yolk with milk; brush 1 tsp (5 mL) over pastry. Sprinkle half with half the bread crumbs, then half the mushroom mixture. Fold uncovered pastry over filling; seal edges. Repeat with remaining ingredients. Cover and refrigerate for at least 1 hour or for up to 24 hours.

● Brush with remaining glaze, adding more milk if necessary. Score into bite-size squares; slash vents in tops. Bake in 425°F (220°C) oven for 20 to 25 minutes or until golden. Let stand for 10 minutes. Cut into squares. Makes 48 hors d'oeuvres.

If cultivated exotic mushrooms such as shiitake, oyster, portobello or crimini are unavailable or threaten to break the budget, rest assured these squares are still utterly delicious made with 1-3/4 lb (875 g) regular white mushrooms (agaracus).

Per hors d'oeuvre: about
- 60 calories
- 4 g fat
- 1 g protein
- 5 g carbohydrate

Calico Mussels

3 lb	mussels	1.5 kg
1/2 cup	dry white wine or water	125 mL
1	small onion, minced	1
1	lemon, cut in wedges	1
1/4 cup	olive oil	50 mL
3	cloves garlic, minced	3
1/4 cup	chopped fresh parsley	50 mL
3 tbsp	red wine vinegar	50 mL
Half	each sweet red and yellow pepper, diced	Half
1	small carrot, shredded	1
1/4 tsp	pepper	1 mL
Pinch	salt	Pinch
	Shredded lettuce	

● Scrub mussels, removing beards. Discard any that do not close when tapped. In saucepan, bring wine, onion and 1 lemon wedge to simmer over medium-high heat. Add mussels; cover and steam until mussels open, about 5 minutes. Discard any that do not open. Transfer to bowl. Boil liquid for 5 to 7 minutes or until reduced to 1/2 cup (125 mL). Discard lemon.

● In skillet, heat oil over medium heat; cook garlic for 2 minutes. Add reduced liquid, parsley, vinegar, sweet peppers, carrot, pepper and salt; pour into separate bowl.

● Remove mussels from shells and add to marinade in bowl. Reserve half of each shell. Cover and refrigerate mussels and shells for at least 2 hours or preferably for 24 hours. Arrange shells on lettuce-lined plate; fill each with mussel. Spoon marinade over top; garnish with remaining lemon. Makes 60 hors d'oeuvres.

Mussels are the affordable yet impressive seafood on any menu. Marinating the mollusks a day ahead boosts their appealing flavor.

Per hors d'oeuvre: about
- 20 calories
- 1 g fat
- 1 g protein
- 1 g carbohydrate

M E N U
SPECIAL FOR SUNDAY
We've added a dash of new flavors to a time-honored menu and the pleasures of Sunday dinner with family and friends.

LEEK AND WATERCRESS CONSOMMÉ
HERBED ROAST OF BEEF WITH HORSERADISH CREAM SAUCE
ONION MASHED SWEET POTATOES
STEAMED BRUSSELS SPROUTS
RED AND GREEN SALAD WITH SHERRY VINAIGRETTE

Herbed Roast Beef with Horseradish Cream Sauce

1	prime rib roast (about 5 lb/2.5 kg)	1
1	clove garlic, slivered	1
1 tbsp	each dried oregano and basil	15 mL
1-1/2 tsp	dried mint	7 mL
1 tsp	pepper	5 mL
2 tbsp	olive oil	25 mL
	Horseradish Cream Sauce (recipe follows)	

● Cut slits all over roast; insert garlic slivers. In small bowl, combine oregano, basil, mint and pepper; stir in oil until pastelike. Spread all over top and sides of roast.

● Place roast, bone side down, on greased rack in roasting pan. Roast in 325°F (160°C) oven for about 2 hours or until meat thermometer registers 140°F (60°C) for rare, or for about 2-1/2 hours or until meat thermometer registers 150°F (65°C) for medium-rare.

● Transfer roast to cutting board and tent with foil; let stand for 15 minutes before carving. Serve with Horseradish Cream Sauce. Makes 6 to 8 servings.

HORSERADISH CREAM SAUCE		
3 tbsp	prepared horseradish	50 mL
1/2 cup	light sour cream	125 mL
1 tsp	Dijon mustard	5 mL

● In small sieve, gently press out moisture from horseradish. In bowl, stir together horseradish, sour cream and mustard. *(Sauce can be covered and refrigerated for up to 2 days.)* Makes about 2/3 cup (150 mL).

TIP: When buying a roast, look for lightly marbled meat with a uniform color and a thin layer of fat on top. For a beautiful presentation and easier carving, choose a chef's cut that has had the cap meat removed. Some chef's cuts may also have the bones removed, then tied back onto the meat for easier carving.

Sunday dinner calls for the very best roast — and here it is, with an herbed coating and a creamy horseradish sauce.

Per each of 8 servings (with sauce): about
- 315 calories
- 40 g protein
- 15 g fat
- 2 g carbohydrate
- good source of iron

STEAMED BRUSSELS SPROUTS
Trim off wilted or coarse outer leaves from 2 lb (1 kg) brussels sprouts; rinse sprouts. Cut thin end off each stem and score shallow X in bottom. Steam for 10 to 15 minutes, depending on size, or until tender with slightly crunchy center. Or boil, covered, in 2 inches (5 cm) water for 10 to 15 minutes; drain well. Toss with 1 tbsp (15 mL) maple syrup. Season with salt and pepper to taste. Makes 8 servings.

Leek and Watercress Consommé

A consommé is an easy, sophisticated way to start a meal. This one is flecked with tiny pieces of leek and peppery watercress.

Per each of 8 servings: about
- 55 calories
- 4 g protein
- 3 g fat
- 3 g carbohydrate

2	small leeks	2
2 tsp	sesame oil	10 mL
1 tsp	vegetable oil	5 mL
2 tsp	minced gingerroot	10 mL
6 cups	chicken stock	1.5 L
Dash	hot pepper sauce	Dash
1 cup	watercress leaves	250 mL

● Cut off green part from leeks. Slit to root and rinse under cold running water; slice thinly. In saucepan, heat sesame and vegetable oils over medium heat; cook leeks and ginger, stirring occasionally, for 5 minutes or until softened.

● Pour in chicken stock and hot pepper sauce; bring to boil. Reduce heat and simmer for 15 minutes. Stir in watercress. Makes 6 to 8 servings.

Onion Mashed Sweet Potatoes

Cooking the onions slowly brings out their sweetness and softens them enough to purée along with the sweet potatoes. This make-ahead dish reheats handily in the microwave.

Per each of 8 servings: about
- 190 calories
- 3 g protein
- 6 g fat
- 31 g carbohydrate

3 tbsp	butter	50 mL
2 tsp	olive oil	10 mL
1	large onion, chopped	1
1 tsp	each salt and pepper	5 mL
1 tsp	Worcestershire sauce	5 mL
3 lb	sweet potatoes (about 6)	1.5 kg
3/4 cup	milk	175 mL

● In nonstick skillet, melt 1 tbsp (15 mL) of the butter with oil over medium-high heat; cook onion and 3/4 tsp (4 mL) each of the salt and pepper, stirring, for 2 minutes. Reduce heat to medium-low; cook, stirring occasionally, for 30 minutes or until onions are very soft and starting to caramelize. Stir in Worcestershire sauce; cook for 10 minutes, stirring often.

● Meanwhile, peel and cut sweet potatoes into chunks. In large pot of boiling salted water, cover and cook potatoes for about 20 minutes or until very tender; drain well.

● In food processor, combine potatoes, onion mixture, milk and remaining butter, salt and pepper; using on/off motion, purée until smooth. (Potatoes can be transferred to 8-inch/2 L square baking dish, covered and refrigerated for up to 1 day. To reheat, microwave at Medium-High/70% power for about 8 minutes.) Makes 6 to 8 servings.

Red and Green Salad with Sherry Vinaigrette

This festive salad makes a refreshing accompaniment to the rest of the meal. For the best flavor, use extra virgin olive oil.

Per serving: about
- 95 calories
- 1 g protein
- 9 g fat
- 3 g carbohydrate

6 cups	torn romaine lettuce	1.5 L
2 cups	torn radicchio or shredded red cabbage	500 mL
1/2 cup	sliced radishes	125 mL
	VINAIGRETTE	
2 tbsp	sherry vinegar or red wine vinegar	25 mL
1 tbsp	minced green onion	15 mL
1 tbsp	chopped fresh parsley	15 mL
1/4 tsp	dried thyme	1 mL
1/4 tsp	each salt and pepper	1 mL
1/4 tsp	granulated sugar	1 mL
1/4 cup	olive oil	50 mL

● VINAIGRETTE: In bowl, whisk together vinegar, onion, parsley, thyme, salt, pepper and sugar; gradually whisk in oil. (Viniaigrette can be refrigerated in covered jar for up to 8 hours. Shake well before using.)

● In salad bowl, toss together romaine, radicchio and radishes. Pour vinaigrette over top; toss well to coat. Makes 6 servings.

MENU

ALOHA! TROPICAL TASTES

You won't have to worry about booking airline tickets when you wing your way to the land of palm trees, sunny skies and golden beaches with this nouveau Hawaiian menu!

GOLDEN CURRY ROASTED NUTS
GINGER-GLAZED PORK TENDERLOINS
CITRUS SWEET POTATOES
SWEET ONION STIR-FRY

Golden Curry Roasted Nuts

2 tsp	liquid honey	10 mL
1 tsp	butter	5 mL
3/4 tsp	curry powder	4 mL
1/2 tsp	ground cumin	2 mL
1/4 tsp	salt	1 mL
8 oz	unsalted macadamia or whole cashew nuts	250 g

● In saucepan or microwaveable bowl, heat honey, butter, curry powder, cumin and salt over low heat until blended; add nuts, stirring to coat well.

● Spread in single layer on baking sheet; bake in 325°F (160°C) oven, stirring frequently, for 10 to 15 minutes or until lightly roasted and fragrant. Let cool completely. *(Nuts can be stored in airtight container for up to 2 days.)* Makes 3 cups (750 mL).

With a gentle curry come-on, these crunchy roasted nuts are just enough to whet your appetite for the feast to follow.

Per 1/4 cup (50 mL): about
- 140 calories
- 2 g protein
- 14 g fat
- 4 g carbohydrate

Ginger-Glazed Pork Tenderloins

1/4 cup	thinly sliced green onions	50 mL
2 tbsp	grated gingerroot	25 mL
2 tbsp	soy sauce	25 mL
2 tbsp	liquid honey	25 mL
1 tbsp	molasses	15 mL
2	small cloves garlic, minced	2
1/2 tsp	salt	2 mL
1/4 tsp	pepper	1 mL
2	large pork tenderloins (12 oz/375 g each), trimmed	2

● In large bowl, combine green onions, ginger, soy sauce, honey, molasses, garlic, salt and pepper; add pork, turning to coat well. Cover and refrigerate for at least 4 hours or for up to 8 hours.

● Reserving marinade, place pork on foil-lined rimmed baking sheet; broil 6 inches (15 cm) from heat, basting once with marinade, for about 20 minutes or until juices run clear when pork is pierced and just a hint of pink remains inside. Transfer to cutting board and tent with foil; let stand for 10 minutes before carving. Makes 6 servings.

Even the avid cook will enjoy the ease of these impressive boneless pork tenderloins. They're marinated for the day in fresh ginger, soy sauce and honey, then finished off with a fuss-free stint under the broiler.

Per serving: about
- 175 calories
- 24 g protein
- 4 g fat
- 10 g carbohydrate

Citrus Sweet Potatoes

Three different citrus juices meld in these tangy glazed sweet potatoes. For fun, you can garnish with sweet potato slices cut into palm trees or sun umbrellas (use a knife or cookie cutter).

Per serving: about
- 220 calories
- 4 g fat
- high source of fiber
- 2 g protein
- 45 g carbohydrate

2 lb	sweet potatoes (4)	1 kg
1 tbsp	grated orange rind	15 mL
1/3 cup	orange juice	75 mL
1/3 cup	grapefruit juice	75 mL
1/4 cup	packed brown sugar	50 mL
2 tbsp	butter, melted	25 mL
2 tbsp	lemon juice	25 mL
1 tsp	salt	5 mL
1/2 tsp	pepper	2 mL

● Peel and slice potatoes 1/4- inch (5 mm) thick; overlap in single layer in 13- x 9-inch (3 L) baking dish. Combine orange rind and juice, grapefruit juice, sugar, butter, lemon juice, salt and pepper; pour evenly over sweet potatoes. Cover and bake in 375°F (190°C) oven for 40 minutes. Uncover and bake, basting every 10 minutes, for about 30 minutes longer or until tender and glazed. Makes 6 servings.

Sweet Onion Stir-Fry

Hawaii is famous for its sweet Maui onions. You can almost duplicate their flavor at home by cooking onions slowly to bring out their sweetness before sautéeing them with the broccoli and red peppers.

Per serving: about
- 100 calories
- 5 g fat
- 3 g protein
- 12 g carbohydrate

1	Spanish onion	1
2 tbsp	vegetable oil	25 mL
1 tsp	each granulated sugar, salt and red wine vinegar	5 mL
3	cloves garlic, minced	3
6 cups	broccoli florets	1.5 L
1/2 cup	vegetable stock or water	125 mL
2	sweet red peppers, sliced	2
1/2 tsp	pepper	2 mL

● Cut onion in half lengthwise; cut crosswise into 1/2-inch (1 cm) thick slices. In skillet, heat oil over medium-low heat; cook onion, sugar, 1/2 tsp (2 mL) of the salt, the vinegar and garlic, covered and stirring occasionally, for 20 minutes or until translucent but not browned. Remove from pan; set aside.

● Add broccoli, stock, red peppers, pepper and remaining salt. Return onions to pan; cover and cook over high heat, until broccoli is tender-crisp. Makes 6 servings.

Pesto Pork Roast

1	loin rack of pork (3 lb/1.5 kg)	1
1	clove garlic, slivered	1
1/4 tsp	each salt and pepper	1 mL
	PESTO	
1 cup	packed fresh basil leaves	250 mL
1/4 cup	freshly grated Parmesan cheese	50 mL
2 tbsp	pine nuts	25 mL
1/3 cup	olive oil	75 mL
2	cloves garlic, minced	2
1/4 tsp	pepper	1 mL
Pinch	salt	Pinch

● Cut tiny slits all over pork; insert garlic slivers. Sprinkle with salt and pepper.

● Turn off burner on one side of barbecue. Place pork, rib ends up, on greased grill over indirect heat (see box, p. 32). Close lid and cook over medium heat for 1-1/2 hours.

● PESTO: In food processor, finely chop basil, Parmesan cheese and pine nuts. With motor running, gradually add oil in thin steady stream until thick paste forms. Stir in garlic, pepper and salt.

● Remove half of the pesto and brush over pork; cover remaining pesto and set aside. Cook pork, covered, for about 1 hour longer or until meat thermometer registers 160°F (70°C).

● Transfer pork to cutting board and tent with foil; let stand for 10 minutes. Slice between bones into individual portions. Serve with reserved pesto. Makes 8 servings.

T*o cut this rack of pork neatly into chop-size slices, have the butcher chine the rack — that is, remove the backbone.*

Per serving: about
- 365 calories
- 26 g protein
- 28 g fat
- 1 g carbohydrate

ASPARAGUS BUNDLES

Asparagus bundles absorb wonderful flavor from the grill. Offer up one of the best tastes of spring and summer in an unusual but delectable way.

● Snap off tough ends of 1 lb (500 g) pencil-thin asparagus and discard. Divide stalks into 4 equal piles. Cut quarter of sweet red pepper into thin strips; divide evenly on top of asparagus. Top each pile with rosemary sprig.

● Using 10-inch (25 cm) length of soaked kitchen string, tie each pile into bundle. Brush 1 tbsp (15 mL) butter evenly over bundles; sprinkle with salt and pepper. Place on greased grill over medium-high heat; close lid and cook, turning once, for about 10 minutes or until asparagus is tender-crisp. Makes 4 servings.

Per serving: about • 50 calories • 2 g protein • 3 g fat • 4 g carbohydrate

Let's Go Casual

Cozy up to the weekend with some easy get-togethers, the kind of invitations everyone loves to get, whether they're planned or impromptu. "Nothing elaborate" and "make ahead" are perfect words for this style of entertaining and the easy-on-the-cook recipes in this chapter.

Baked Rigatoni and Meatballs ▶

Meatballs can be made with either lean ground turkey, chicken or beef in this ever-pleasing baked pasta dish.

Per serving: about
- 780 calories
- 34 g fat
- very high source of fiber
- 49 g protein
- 70 g carbohydrate
- excellent source of calcium and iron

2 tbsp	olive oil	25 mL
1	onion, chopped	1
2	cloves garlic, minced	2
3 cups	sliced mushrooms (8 oz/250 g)	750 mL
1	sweet green pepper, chopped	1
1-1/2 tsp	each dried basil and granulated sugar	7 mL
1 tsp	each dried oregano and salt	5 mL
3/4 tsp	pepper	4 mL
1	can (28 oz/796 mL) tomatoes, chopped	1
2 tbsp	tomato paste	25 mL
3-1/2 cups	rigatoni pasta (8 oz/250 g)	875 mL
1-1/3 cups	shredded part-skim mozzarella cheese	325 mL
1/4 cup	freshly grated Parmesan cheese	50 mL
	MEATBALLS	
1	egg	1
1/3 cup	finely chopped onion	75 mL
1/4 cup	dry bread crumbs	50 mL
2	cloves garlic, minced	2
3 tbsp	freshly grated Parmesan cheese	45 mL
1 tsp	dried oregano	5 mL
3/4 tsp	salt	4 mL
1/2 tsp	pepper	2 mL
1 lb	lean ground turkey	500 g

● MEATBALLS: In bowl, lightly beat egg; mix in onion, bread crumbs, garlic, Parmesan cheese, oregano, salt and pepper. Mix in turkey. Shape heaping tablespoonfuls (15 mL) into balls.

● In large skillet, heat oil over medium-high heat; cook meatballs, in batches if necessary, for 8 to 10 minutes or until browned all over. Transfer to paper towel-lined plate.

● To skillet, add onion, garlic, mushrooms, green pepper, basil, sugar, oregano, salt, pepper and 2 tbsp (25 mL) water; cook over medium heat, stirring occasionally, for about 10 minutes or until vegetables are softened.

● Stir in tomatoes and tomato paste; bring to boil. Add meatballs; reduce heat and simmer for 30 minutes or until sauce is slightly thickened.

● Meanwhile, in large pot of boiling salted water, cook rigatoni for 8 to 10 minutes or until tender but firm. Drain well and return to pot; add sauce, stirring gently to coat.

● Transfer pasta mixture to 11- x 7-inch (2 L) baking dish or 8-cup (2 L) shallow oval casserole. Sprinkle with mozzarella and Parmesan cheeses. Bake in 400°F (200°C) oven for about 20 minutes or until bubbling, cheese is melted and top is golden. Makes 4 servings.

Polenta with Tomato Sauce ▲

Polenta would be bland if it didn't have a topping such as this herbed vegetarian tomato sauce. The recipe comes from the kitchen of one of Canadian Living's most faithful readers, Montrealer Liliana Tommasini.

Per serving: about
- 190 calories
- 8 g protein
- 5 g fat
- 29 g carbohydrate

1 cup	cornmeal	250 mL
1 tsp	vegetable oil	5 mL
Pinch	salt	Pinch
2/3 cup	shredded part-skim mozzarella cheese	150 mL
1 tbsp	freshly grated Parmesan cheese	15 mL
	TOMATO SAUCE	
1-1/2 tsp	olive oil	7 mL
Half	Spanish onion, finely chopped	Half
2	cloves garlic, minced	2
1	carrot, finely chopped	1
1	can (28 oz/796 mL) tomatoes	1
2 tsp	dried basil	10 mL
1 tsp	dried oregano	5 mL
1/4 tsp	each salt and pepper	1 mL
Pinch	granulated sugar	Pinch

● TOMATO SAUCE: In large saucepan, heat oil over medium heat; cook onion, garlic and carrot, stirring occasionally, for 5 minutes. In food processor, chop tomatoes with juices. Add to saucepan along with basil, oregano, salt, pepper and sugar; bring to boil. Reduce heat and simmer, stirring often, for 1 hour or until thickened.

● Meanwhile, in microwaveable 12-cup (3 L) casserole, stir together 3-1/2 cups (875 mL) water, cornmeal, oil and salt; cover and microwave at High, whisking occasionally, for about 12 minutes or until thickened.

● Spread cornmeal mixture in lightly greased 11- x 7-inch (2 L) baking dish. Spread tomato sauce over top; sprinkle with mozzarella and Parmesan cheeses. Bake in 350°F (180°C) oven for 15 minutes or until sauce and cheese are bubbly. Broil for 2 minutes or until golden brown. Makes 6 servings.

Crusty Puttanesca

1 tsp	olive oil	5 mL
3	cloves garlic, minced	3
1	onion, chopped	1
1-1/2 tsp	each dried basil and oregano	7 mL
1-1/4 tsp	salt	6 mL
1 tsp	granulated sugar	5 mL
1/2 tsp	pepper	2 mL
1/4 tsp	hot pepper flakes	1 mL
1/2 cup	chopped pitted oil-cured olives	125 mL
3 tbsp	capers	45 mL
1	eggplant, peeled and cubed	1
2	cans (28 oz/796 mL each) tomatoes, chopped	2
3 tbsp	tomato paste	45 mL
4 cups	radiatore or fusilli pasta (12 oz/375 g)	1 L
1 cup	shredded part-skim mozzarella cheese	250 mL
1/4 cup	freshly grated Parmesan cheese	50 mL

● In Dutch oven, heat oil over medium heat; cook garlic and onion, stirring occasionally, for about 3 minutes or just until softened. Stir in basil, oregano, salt, sugar, pepper and hot pepper flakes. Add olives, capers and eggplant; cook for 1 minute.

● Pour in 1/2 cup (125 mL) water; cover and cook, stirring occasionally, for about 8 minutes or until eggplant is tender.

● Stir in tomatoes and tomato paste; bring to boil. Reduce heat and simmer, uncovered and stirring occasionally, for 30 minutes.

● Meanwhile, in large pot of boiling salted water, cook pasta for 8 to 10 minutes or until tender but firm. Drain well and add to sauce, stirring to coat. Sprinkle with mozzarella and Parmesan cheeses.

● Bake in 375°F (190°C) oven for about 20 minutes or until cheese is melted and becoming golden. Let stand for 10 minutes. Makes 6 servings.

A *quick, saucy pasta toss is transformed into an al forno, or baked, one-dish dinner. Short pastas such as radiatore or fusilli are the right choice for this dish because their curly shapes entrap the rich mellow tomato sauce and keep the dish luscious and moist under the crusty cheese topping.*

Per serving: about
- 420 calories
- 11 g fat
- very high source of fiber
- good source of iron
- 18 g protein
- 64 g carbohydrate
- excellent source of calcium

Rigatoni with Sweet Peppers

2	sweet red peppers	2
3-1/2 cups	rigatoni pasta (8 oz/250 g)	875 mL
2	cloves garlic, minced	2
2 tbsp	olive oil	25 mL
3 cups	arugula or watercress leaves (about 1 bunch)	750 mL
12	black olives	12
	Pepper	
1/2 cup	freshly grated Parmesan cheese	125 mL

● Broil red peppers, turning often, for 20 minutes or until charred; let cool. Peel off blackened skin; cut in half, core and seed, reserving juice. Cut into strips. Set aside.

● In large pot of boiling salted water, cook rigatoni for 8 to 10 minutes or until tender but firm; drain well.

● Meanwhile, in small microwaveable dish, microwave garlic with oil at High for 1 minute.

● In large bowl, combine garlic mixture, red peppers, arugula and olives. Add pasta; toss well. Add enough of the reserved pepper juice to moisten pasta. Season with pepper to taste. Sprinkle with Parmesan cheese; toss to combine. Makes 4 servings.

I*t's hard to call this quick mix of garlic-infused olive oil, fresh arugula and roasted sweet peppers a sauce, but that's how the combo works with pasta. This recipe is an excellent example of how to use a modest amount of higher-fat ingredients, such as oil and cheese, to maximum taste effect.*

Per serving: about
- 370 calories
- 14 g fat
- 14 g protein
- 48 g carbohydrate

TIP: When draining cooked pasta, save up to 1 cup (250 mL) of the cooking liquid. Some can be added, if needed, to moisten pasta without pouring on extra oil or other high-fat ingredients.

Turkey Piccata ▲

*T*hin slices of lean turkey replace veal in this Canadian version of a lemony Italian classic.

Per serving: about
- 210 calories
- 29 g protein
- 7 g fat
- 4 g carbohydrate

1	egg	1
1/2 cup	all-purpose flour	125 mL
2 tsp	grated lemon rind	10 mL
1/2 tsp	each salt and dried thyme	2 mL
1/4 tsp	pepper	1 mL
1 lb	turkey scallopini	500 g
2 tsp	each butter and olive oil	10 mL
	Chopped fresh parsley	

● In shallow dish, lightly beat egg. In separate shallow dish, combine flour, lemon rind, salt, thyme and pepper. Dip turkey into egg to coat well; press into flour mixture, turning to coat all over.

● In nonstick skillet, heat half each of the butter and oil over medium heat; cook half of the turkey, turning once, for 6 minutes or until no longer pink inside. Repeat with remaining butter, oil and turkey. Serve garnished with parsley. Makes 4 servings.

TIP: If turkey scallopini is unavailable, turn 1 lb (500 g) turkey cutlets into thin pieces by pounding between waxed paper with mallet to 1/4-inch (5 mm) thickness.

Cheesy Turkey Casserole

3/4 cup	dry bread crumbs	175 mL
2 tbsp	freshly grated Parmesan cheese	25 mL
1/4 tsp	each salt, pepper and dried basil	1 mL
2	egg whites	2
1 lb	turkey scallopini	500 g
2 tsp	olive oil	10 mL
2 tsp	butter	10 mL
1/2 cup	shredded Asiago cheese	125 mL

EGGPLANT TOMATO SAUCE		
1	eggplant	1
1 tbsp	olive oil	15 mL
1	onion, chopped	1
2	cloves garlic, minced	2
1	can (28 oz/796 mL) stewed tomatoes	1
1 tsp	dried basil	5 mL
3/4 tsp	granulated sugar	4 mL
1/2 tsp	dried oregano	2 mL
1/4 tsp	pepper	1 mL

● EGGPLANT TOMATO SAUCE: Peel and chop eggplant. In heavy saucepan, heat oil over medium heat; cook eggplant, onion and garlic, stirring often, for about 5 minutes or until softened. Add tomatoes, breaking up with spoon; add basil, sugar, oregano and pepper. Bring to boil; reduce heat and simmer, stirring occasionally, for about 15 minutes or until thickened. *(Sauce can be refrigerated in airtight container for up to 3 days.)*

● Meanwhile, in bowl, combine bread crumbs, Parmesan cheese, salt, pepper and basil. In separate bowl, whisk egg whites until foamy. Cut turkey into serving-size portions; dip into egg whites, then into crumb mixture, turning to coat all over.

● In large nonstick skillet, heat 1 tsp (5 mL) each of the oil and butter over medium-high heat; cook half of the turkey, turning once, for 4 minutes or until browned. Repeat with remaining oil, butter and turkey.

● Pour sauce into shallow 10-cup (2.5 L) casserole dish; arrange turkey in single layer over sauce. Sprinkle with Asiago cheese. Cover with foil. Bake in 350°F (180°C) oven for about 25 minutes or until turkey is tender and sauce is bubbly. Uncover and broil for 2 minutes or until cheese is bubbly. Makes 4 servings.

Turkey scallopini with a zesty tomato sauce makes for a light but hearty casserole. For really good cheese flavor, use a small amount of a robust cheese, such as Asiago, instead of a large quantity of bland, lower-fat cheese.

Per serving: about
- 440 calories
- 15 g fat
- high source of fiber
- 39 g protein
- 39 g carbohydrate
- excellent source of calcium and iron

Thai Honey Chicken

4	chicken breasts, skinned (1-1/2 lb/750 g)	4
3	cloves garlic, minced	3
2 tbsp	liquid honey	25 mL
2 tbsp	soy sauce	25 mL
2 tsp	chili paste	10 mL

● Arrange chicken, bone side down, in single layer in shallow baking dish. Score meaty side a few times.

● Combine garlic, honey, soy sauce and chili paste; spread over chicken. Cover and refrigerate for at least 6 hours or for up to 12 hours.

● Bake in 375°F (190°C) oven, turning once and basting occasionally, for 30 to 40 minutes or until no longer pink inside. Strain juices through fine sieve; serve with chicken. Makes 4 servings.

Fans of Chinese honey garlic chicken will enjoy this spicy Thai twist.

Per serving: about
- 170 calories
- 2 g fat
- 28 g protein
- 10 g carbohydrate

Coq au Vin ▶

White wine makes a burnished sauce for this easy version of French chicken in wine. Complement the dish with egg noodles, rice or a crusty baguette to mop up all the delicious sauce.

Per serving: about
- 490 calories
- 44 g protein
- 27 g fat
- 15 g carbohydrate
- excellent source of iron

3-1/2 lb	chicken pieces	1.75 kg
2	onions	2
2	slices bacon, chopped	2
3	cloves garlic, minced	3
1 lb	mushrooms, quartered	500 g
3	carrots, cut in bite-size pieces	3
1 tsp	each dried thyme and salt	5 mL
1/2 tsp	pepper	2 mL
1/4 cup	all-purpose flour	50 mL
1-1/2 cups	dry white wine	375 mL
1 cup	chicken stock	250 mL
1	bay leaf	1
	Chopped fresh parsley	

● Separate chicken legs at joint. If breasts are large, cut diagonally in half. Cut onions in half lengthwise; thinly slice crosswise.

● In Dutch oven, cook bacon over medium heat until crisp; using slotted spoon, transfer to plate. Increase heat to medium-high; brown chicken, in batches if necessary, about 10 minutes. Add to plate.

● Add onions and garlic to pan; cook over medium heat, stirring, for 5 minutes, adding up to 2 tbsp (25 mL) water if sticking to bottom. Add mushrooms, carrots, thyme, salt and pepper; cook, stirring often, for 10 minutes or until almost all liquid is evaporated. Stir in flour for 1 minute. Stir in wine, stock and bay leaf; bring to boil

● Nestle chicken into vegetable mixture; sprinkle bacon over top. Reduce heat, cover and simmer for 20 minutes. Uncover and simmer for about 20 minutes or until juices run clear when chicken is pierced.

● Transfer chicken to platter; cover and keep warm. Discard bay leaf. Bring sauce and vegetables to boil; boil, stirring often, for 5 to 10 minutes or until reduced by half. Pour sauce and vegetables over chicken. Sprinkle with parsley. Makes 6 servings.

Spanish Sausage and Chicken

Sausage is preseasoned, so it adds maximum taste to a dish without lengthening the ingredient list. It also happens to go especially well with chicken and the sunny Mediterranean flavors in this easy stew.

Per serving: about
- 445 calories
- 39 g protein
- 26 g fat
- 14 g carbohydrate
- excellent source of iron

4	chicken legs, skinned	4
6 oz	chorizo or other spicy sausage	175 g
1 tbsp	vegetable oil	15 mL
1	onion, chopped	1
1	clove garlic, minced	1
1	small sweet yellow pepper, cut in strips	1
2 tbsp	chopped fresh oregano (or 2 tsp/10 mL dried)	25 mL
1/4 tsp	each salt and pepper	1 mL
1	can (28 oz/796 mL) tomatoes	1
1/4 cup	sliced black olives	50 mL

● Separate chicken legs at joint. Thinly slice sausage. In large nonstick skillet, heat oil over medium-high heat; brown chicken and sausage all over, in batches if necessary, about 10 minutes. Transfer to plate.

● Add onion and garlic to pan; cook over medium heat, stirring often, for about 5 minutes or until softened. Stir in yellow pepper, oregano, salt and pepper; cook for 5 minutes or until peppers are slightly softened.

● Stir in tomatoes, breaking up with spoon; bring to boil. Reduce heat and nestle chicken and sausage in mixture. Cover and simmer for 20 minutes; uncover and simmer for 5 minutes.

● Add olives; cook for 5 minutes or until juices run clear when chicken is pierced. Makes 4 servings.

Taste-of-India Chicken Legs

Here's a gentle introduction to tandoori-style chicken. Serve with rice, steamed spinach and chutney.

Per serving: about
- 205 calories
- 8 g fat
- good source of iron
- 27 g protein
- 6 g carbohydrate

6	chicken legs, skinned	6
2 tsp	ground cumin	10 mL
2 tsp	paprika	10 mL
1 tsp	turmeric	5 mL
1/2 tsp	each cayenne and black pepper	2 mL
1	onion, chopped	1
3	large cloves garlic	3
1/4 cup	lemon juice	50 mL
1 tbsp	vegetable oil	15 mL
2 tsp	granulated sugar	10 mL
1/2 tsp	all-purpose flour	2 mL
1/4 tsp	salt	1 mL
1/4 cup	plain yogurt	50 mL

● Separate chicken legs at joint; place in glass bowl and set aside.

● In skillet, stir together cumin, paprika, turmeric, cayenne and black pepper; cook over medium heat, stirring, for about 40 seconds or until fragrant. Remove from heat. Stir in onion, garlic, lemon juice, oil and sugar; pour over chicken, turning to coat evenly. Cover and refrigerate for 4 hours or for up to 12 hours, turning often.

● Place chicken, meaty side down, in lightly greased roasting pan; pour on marinade. Bake in 400°F (200°C) oven for 20 minutes; turn and bake, basting with pan juices, for about 20 minutes or until crusty outside and juices run clear when chicken is pierced. Transfer chicken to platter; keep warm.

● Set roasting pan over medium-high heat; whisk in flour and bring to boil. Cook, whisking, for 30 to 40 seconds or until thickened. Stir in salt and yogurt (do not boil). Pour sauce over chicken. Makes 6 servings.

Barbecued Chicken with Sage and Parsley

Sage stuffed into the cavity of the bird infuses the meat with fresh herb flavor as the chicken crisps and browns over the coals.

Per serving: about
- 310 calories
- 19 g fat
- 33 g protein
- trace of carbohydrate

3/4 cup	each packed fresh sage and parsley sprigs	175 mL
1	chicken (4 lb/2 kg)	1
1/2 tsp	each salt and pepper	2 mL
Half	lemon	Half
2 tbsp	olive oil	25 mL

● Remove leaves from 1/4 cup (50 mL) of the sage sprigs; chop to make 2 tbsp (25 mL) and set aside. Set remaining sage sprigs and stems aside. Repeat for parsley.

● Remove neck and giblets from chicken. Rinse and pat chicken dry inside and out. Sprinkle cavity with half each of the salt and pepper. Rub outside with lemon, squeezing gently; place lemon shell inside cavity. Stuff with reserved sage and parsley stems and sprigs. Tie legs together with kitchen string; tuck wings under back. Brush with half of the oil; sprinkle with remaining salt, pepper and reserved chopped sage and parsley.

● Place chicken, breast side down, on greased grill over indirect heat (see box, this page). Close lid and cook over medium heat for 15 minutes.

● Turn chicken and brush with remaining oil. Cook, covered, for about 1-1/2 hours or until meat thermometer inserted in thickest part of thigh registers 185°F (85°C). Transfer to cutting board and tent with foil; let stand for 10 minutes before carving. Makes 6 servings.

BARBECUING WITH INDIRECT HEAT

For this method of cooking, the meat is not placed directly over the heat source.
● For a charcoal barbecue: Push hot coals to the sides, place a drip pan in the center of coals and put the chicken or meat on the grill above to cook.
● For a gas or electric barbecue with two burners: Set a drip pan under unlit burner and place the chicken or meat on the rack above. The other burner is lit, providing all the heat needed.

Garlic Chicken Roast

2	whole heads garlic	2
1	chicken (4 lb/2 kg)	1
1/2 tsp	each salt and pepper	2 mL
1 tbsp	olive oil	15 mL
4	carrots, cut in chunks	4
2	onions, quartered	2
2 cups	cubed peeled rutabaga	500 mL
1 tsp	crushed dried rosemary	5 mL
1/2 cup	chicken stock	125 mL
1/3 cup	dry white wine	75 mL
4 tsp	all-purpose flour	20 mL

● Separate heads of garlic into individual cloves; peel and set aside. Remove neck and giblets from chicken. Rinse and pat chicken dry inside and out. Sprinkle inside and out with salt and pepper. Place 2 garlic cloves in cavity. Tie legs together with kitchen string; tuck wings under back. Set aside.

● In large Dutch oven, heat oil over medium heat; cook remaining garlic, carrots, onions, rutabaga and rosemary, stirring often, for 5 minutes. Add stock and wine; bring to boil. Reduce heat and simmer for 3 minutes or until slightly reduced.

● Nestle chicken into vegetables, breast side up; spoon juices over top. Cover and roast in 325°F (160°C) oven, basting occasionally, for 45 minutes. Uncover and roast, basting occasionally, for 2 to 2-1/2 hours longer or until meat thermometer inserted in thickest part of thigh registers 185°F (85°C).

● Transfer chicken to cutting board; tent with foil and let stand for 10 minutes before carving. With slotted spoon, transfer vegetables to serving dish; keep warm.

● Meanwhile, skim fat from pan juices. In jar with tight-fitting lid, shake together flour and 2 tbsp (25 mL) water until smooth; whisk into pan juices and bring to boil. Reduce heat and simmer, stirring, for 3 minutes or until thickened. Serve with chicken and vegetables. Makes 4 servings.

This whole chicken roasts in an aromatic bed of garlic and vegetables. The skin crisps, the vegetables soften to fork-tenderness, and chicken and vegetables are all eaten with a splash of thickened cooking juices.

Per serving: about
- 560 calories
- 29 g fat
- high source of fiber
- 48 g protein
- 4 g carbohydrate
- excellent source of iron

Chicken Tortilla Casserole

1 lb	boneless skinless chicken breasts	500 g
1/4 tsp	each salt and pepper	1 mL
1 tbsp	vegetable oil	15 mL
2	green onions, chopped	2
1	sweet green pepper, chopped	1
1 tsp	chili powder	5 mL
1/4 tsp	ground cumin	1 mL
1	can (19 oz/540 mL) stewed tomatoes	1
4 oz	light cream cheese, cubed	125 g
1 cup	corn kernels	250 mL
10	stale corn tortillas	10
1/2 cup	shredded Monterey Jack cheese	125 mL

● Cut chicken into strips; sprinkle with salt and pepper. In nonstick skillet, heat half of the oil over medium-high heat; cook chicken, in batches if necessary, until browned and no longer pink inside. Transfer to large bowl.

● Heat remaining oil in skillet over medium heat; cook onions, green pepper, chili powder and cumin, stirring occasionally, for about 5 minutes or until onions are softened. Add tomatoes; cook, stirring, for 5 minutes. Stir in cream cheese until blended. Add to chicken along with corn, stirring to combine.

● Meanwhile, break or cut tortillas into small pieces; spread half in greased 8-inch (2 L) square baking dish. Spoon half of the chicken mixture over tortillas. Repeat layers. Sprinkle with Monterey Jack cheese.

● Cover and bake in 350°F (180°C) oven for about 35 minutes or until bubbly. Uncover and broil for 2 minutes or until cheese is golden. Makes 4 servings.

Thrifty cooks in the American Southwest devised this homey yet savory casserole featuring stale corn tortillas.

Per serving: about
- 480 calories
- 18 g fat
- high source of fiber
- 38 g protein
- 43 g carbohydrate
- good source of calcium and iron

TIP: To make tortillas stale, let stand, uncovered, at room temperature for about 2 hours.

Greek Lamb and Onion Stew

Abundant with sweet onions, plumped with tiny pasta and simmered in a tomatoey wine sauce, this savory lamb stew draws its inspiration from the Greek stefado. Get in the Hellenic mood and serve it with a chunky salad of cucumber, tomatoes, onions, feta cheese and black olives, and thick slices of crusty bread.

Per serving: about
- 370 calories
- 29 g protein
- 12 g fat
- 36 g carbohydrate
- excellent source of iron

1-1/2 lb	lean boneless lamb shoulder	750 g
1/4 tsp	each salt and pepper	1 mL
2 tbsp	olive oil	25 mL
6	small onions, quartered	6
3	cloves garlic, minced	3
1	can (19 oz/540 mL) stewed tomatoes	1
1 cup	beef stock	250 mL
1/2 cup	dry red wine or beef stock	125 mL
2 tbsp	tomato paste	25 mL
2	bay leaves	2
1 tsp	dried oregano	5 mL
1/2 tsp	cinnamon	2 mL
1 cup	orzo pasta	250 mL
1/4 cup	chopped fresh parsley	50 mL

● Cut lamb into 1-inch (2.5 cm) cubes; trim off any fat. Sprinkle with salt and pepper.

● In Dutch oven, heat half of the oil over medium-high heat; brown lamb, in batches and adding some of the remaining oil if needed. Transfer to plate.

● Heat remaining oil in pan. Over medium heat, cook onions and garlic, stirring often and adding 2 tbsp (25 mL) water if necessary to prevent sticking, for 5 minutes or until starting to soften.

● Return lamb and accumulated juices to pan. Add tomatoes, stock, wine, tomato paste, bay leaves, oregano and cinnamon; bring to boil, stirring to scrape up brown bits from bottom of pan. Reduce heat, cover and simmer for 1 hour.

● Add orzo; simmer, uncovered, for about 15 minutes or until lamb and pasta are tender. Discard bay leaves. Stir in parsley. Makes 6 servings.

Spicy Orange Pork Ribs

Back ribs or side ribs are both succulent, but side ribs cost less and still offer nice portions of meat. In warm weather, you can glaze and crisp the ribs on the barbecue.

Per serving: about
- 485 calories
- 31 g protein
- 30 g fat
- 21 g carbohydrate
- good source of iron

3 lb	pork side ribs	1.5 kg
1	onion, chopped	1
1	bay leaf	1
	SAUCE	
1 cup	orange juice	250 mL
3 tbsp	liquid honey	50 mL
1 tbsp	each minced gingerroot and soy sauce	15 mL
1 tsp	five-spice powder	5 mL
1	clove garlic, minced	1

● Cut ribs into small sections; trim off fat. In large saucepan, cover ribs with cold water. Add onion and bay leaf; bring to boil. Reduce heat and simmer for 35 to 40 minutes or until fork-tender. Drain; discard onion and bay leaf.

● SAUCE: Meanwhile, in small saucepan, combine orange juice, honey, ginger, soy sauce, five-spice powder and garlic. Bring to boil; reduce heat and simmer for 10 minutes.

● Arrange ribs in single layer in 13- x 9-inch (3 L) baking dish. Spoon sauce over top. Bake in 350°F (180°C) oven, turning twice and basting occasionally, for 30 to 35 minutes or until ribs are glazed and sauce is thickened and sticky. Makes 4 servings.

Sweet Potato and Pork Pie

2 tbsp	vegetable oil	25 mL
1	onion, chopped	1
2	cloves garlic, minced	2
1-1/2 lb	lean ground pork	750 g
1/2 cup	chicken stock	125 mL
1/3 cup	dry sherry or chicken stock	75 mL
1/4 cup	Dijon mustard	50 mL
2 tbsp	chopped fresh parsley	25 mL
1 tsp	each salt and pepper	5 mL
1-1/2 lb	parsnips (about 5)	750 g
1/2 tsp	dried marjoram	2 mL
2 lb	sweet potatoes (about 4)	1 kg
2 tbsp	butter	25 mL
1	egg, lightly beaten	1

● In large saucepan, heat oil over medium heat; cook onion and garlic, stirring occasionally, for 5 minutes or until softened. Add pork; cook, breaking up with spoon, for about 8 minutes or until browned. Drain off fat.

● Stir in stock and sherry; simmer, scraping up brown bits from bottom of pan, for about 10 minutes or until most of the liquid is evaporated. Mix in mustard, parsley and 1/4 tsp (1 mL) each of the salt and pepper. Set aside.

● Peel parsnips; slice into rounds. In saucepan of boiling salted water, cook parsnips for 10 minutes or just until fork-tender; drain. Mix in marjoram and 1/4 tsp (1 mL) each of the salt and pepper. Set aside.

● Peel and quarter potatoes. In saucepan of boiling salted water, cook potatoes for 10 minutes or just until fork-tender. Drain and mash with butter and remaining salt and pepper.

● Arrange parsnips over bottom of 12-cup (3 L) casserole; spoon meat mixture over top. Spoon potatoes over meat; brush with egg. Bake in 425°F (220°C) oven for 15 minutes. Reduce heat to 350°F (180°C); bake for 30 minutes. Let stand for 10 minutes. Makes 6 servings.

Shepherd's pie with a twist — pork to replace the lamb or beef, and orange sweet potatoes instead of white spuds to fluff over the top. This recipe, from Laurel Kreuger of Baker Lake, Northwest Territories, appeared in Canadian Living's *twentieth anniversary issue.*

Per serving: about
- 585 calories
- 30 g fat
- very high source of fiber
- 27 g protein
- 52 g carbohydrate
- good source of iron

Sausage Chili

1-1/2 lb	mild Italian sausage	750 g
3	onions, chopped	3
3	cloves garlic, minced	3
1	each sweet red and green pepper, chopped	1
1-1/2 cups	chopped celery	375 mL
1 tbsp	chili powder	15 mL
1 tsp	each ground cumin and dried oregano	5 mL
1/2 tsp	salt	2 mL
1/4 tsp	pepper	1 mL
2	cans (19 oz/540 mL each) tomatoes	2
2	cans (19 oz/540 mL each) red kidney beans, drained and rinsed	2
1	can (14 oz/398 mL) tomato sauce	1
1/4 cup	chopped fresh parsley	50 mL

● Cut sausage into 1/2-inch (1 cm) thick slices. In large saucepan or Dutch oven, cook sausage over medium-high heat, stirring occasionally, for 12 to 15 minutes or until browned. Remove and drain on paper towels.

● Drain off all but 1 tbsp (15 mL) fat from pan. Reduce heat to medium; cook onions, garlic, red and green peppers and celery, stirring occasionally, for 5 minutes. Add chili powder, cumin, oregano, salt and pepper; cook, stirring, for 1 minute.

● Stir in tomatoes, breaking up with spoon. Return sausage to pan; add kidney beans and tomato sauce. Bring to boil; reduce heat and simmer for 40 to 45 minutes or until thickened. Stir in parsley. *(Chili can be refrigerated in airtight container for up to 3 days.)* Makes 8 servings.

Planning ahead with a dish such as this is a great way to get two meals out of one. Invite company to enjoy this pleasingly spicy chili served with whole wheat rolls and a salad, then roll up leftovers in tortillas the next night.

Per serving: about
- 365 calories
- 15 g fat
- very high source of fiber
- 23 g protein
- 38 g carbohydrate
- excellent source of iron

Caribbean Salmon on Rice and Beans

There's a hint of Jamaica in every bite of this succulent salmon — from the touch of thyme, curry and hot sauce to the rice and beans, of course, and the thick wedge of orange we suggest you squeeze over each portion.

Per serving: about
- 635 calories
- 3 g fat
- high source of fiber
- 41 g protein
- 67 g carbohydrate
- good source of iron

1 lb	salmon fillet (with skin)	500 g
Pinch	salt	Pinch
1 cup	parboiled rice	250 mL
Pinch	dried thyme	Pinch
1	can (19 oz/540 mL) red kidney beans, drained and rinsed	1
1	small mango, peach or nectarine, peeled and diced	1
	Lettuce leaves	
	DRESSING	
1 tsp	coarsely grated orange rind	5 mL
1/2 cup	orange juice	125 mL
1/4 cup	vegetable oil	50 mL
3 tbsp	lime or lemon juice	50 mL
2	large green onions, chopped	2
2	cloves garlic, minced	2
3/4 tsp	curry powder	4 mL
1/2 tsp	each salt, pepper, dried thyme and hot pepper sauce	2 mL

● DRESSING: In small bowl, whisk together orange rind and juice, oil, lime juice, onions, garlic, curry powder, salt, pepper, thyme and hot pepper sauce.

● Cut salmon crosswise into 2-inch (5 cm) wide strips. Place, skin side down, in glass dish just big enough to hold in single layer. Remove 2 tbsp (25 mL) of the dressing; brush over fish. Let stand for 30 minutes at room temperature.

● Meanwhile, in saucepan, bring 2 cups (500 mL) water and salt to boil; add rice and thyme. Reduce heat to low; cover and cook for about 20 minutes or until rice is tender and water is absorbed. Fluff with fork; pour in all but 1 tbsp (15 mL) of the dressing. Add kidney beans and mango; toss gently with fork to combine.

● Place salmon, skin side down, on greased grill over medium-high heat; cook, without turning, for 7 to 10 minutes or just until fish flakes easily when tested with fork.

● Line plates with lettuce; mound rice mixture on top. Using metal spatula, carefully lift salmon off skin; place on top of rice. Drizzle with remaining dressing. Makes 4 servings.

SUBSTITUTIONS FOR PANTRY ITEMS

When substituting ingredients, the taste of the finished dish won't be exactly the same but it will still be delicious and as faithful to the flavors as possible.

● **Balsamic Vinegar:** Use same quantity of red wine vinegar, with a pinch of granulated sugar.

● **White Wine Vinegar:** Real apple cider vinegar and lemon juice are good choices.

If color isn't important, substitute red wine vinegar.

● **Chili Paste:** Hot pepper sauce is always handy, or use a careful amount of cayenne pepper.

● **Wine:** Stock, either beef for red wine or chicken for white, is the most successful substitute. Since stock is saltier than wine, add any salt to recipe at end of cooking time. Avoid substituting stock in dishes that need to be boiled down, since reduction intensifies saltiness. You will need to balance the dish with a dash of vinegar at end of cooking time.

● **Thai Fish Sauce:** Use light (not low-sodium, light-colored) soy sauce.

● **Dijon Mustard:** Use a third of the amount of dry mustard or, if a sweet flavor is called for, Russian-style prepared mustard.

● **Pasta:** Most short and long pastas are usually interchangeable.

● **Beans:** Most beans and chick-peas are usually interchangeable in chilis, stews, salads and dips. Some come in colors that contrast more appealingly — and the trendy one, black beans, brings new zing to chili.

Shrimp Casserole Sees the Light ▾

3/4 cup	long-grain rice	175 mL
1	egg white	1
1/4 cup	chopped fresh parsley	50 mL
3 tbsp	butter	50 mL
1	clove garlic, minced	1
2 cups	sliced mushrooms (about 6 oz/175 g)	500 mL
1 cup	sliced celery	250 mL
1/2 cup	chopped green onions	125 mL
1/2 tsp	dried dillweed	2 mL
1/2 tsp	each salt and pepper	2 mL
1 lb	raw unpeeled shrimp	500 g
3 tbsp	all-purpose flour	50 mL
1-1/2 cups	milk	375 mL
3/4 cup	shredded Gruyère cheese	175 mL
2 tsp	grated lemon rind	10 mL
1/4 cup	fresh bread crumbs	50 mL

● In saucepan, bring 1-1/2 cups (375 mL) salted water to boil; add rice. Reduce heat to low; cover and cook for 15 to 20 minutes or until rice is tender and water is absorbed. Remove from heat. Stir in egg white and 1 tbsp (15 mL) of the parsley. Press over bottom of greased 8-inch (2 L) square baking dish or shallow heatproof casserole with same volume; set aside.

● Meanwhile, in nonstick skillet, melt 1 tbsp (15 mL) of the butter over medium-high heat; cook garlic, mushrooms and celery, stirring occasionally, for about 5 minutes or just until beginning to brown. Stir in onions, dill and 1/4 tsp (1 mL) each of the salt and pepper; cook over high heat for about 2 minutes or until lightly browned. Transfer to large bowl.

● Wipe out skillet. Pour in 2 cups (500 mL) water and bring to simmer; add shrimp and cook for about 1 minute or just until pink. Reserving 1 cup (250 mL) of the liquid, cool shrimp under cold water. Peel and devein shrimp; arrange over rice in baking dish.

● In heavy saucepan, melt remaining butter over medium heat; stir in flour and cook, stirring, for 2 minutes, without browning.

Gradually whisk in reserved shrimp liquid and milk; cook, stirring, for about 20 minutes or until thickened. Remove from heat. Stir in 1/2 cup (125 mL) of the Gruyère cheese, lemon rind and remaining salt and pepper until cheese is melted. Stir into vegetable mixture along with remaining parsley; pour over shrimp in baking dish. *(Casserole can be prepared to this point, covered and then refrigerated for up to 1 day.)*

● In small bowl, stir together remaining cheese and bread crumbs. Sprinkle evenly over casserole. Bake in 325°F (160°C) oven for about 45 minutes or until bubbly. Broil for about 2 minutes or until top is golden. Let stand for 15 minutes. Makes 4 servings.

T*his lightened version of an all-time favorite casserole can be made with any combination of seafood — scallops, crab or lobster, even chunks of fresh salmon.*

Per serving: about
- 480 calories
- 19 g fat
- excellent source of calcium
- 32 g protein
- 43 g carbohydrate
- good source of iron

Monkfish Stew

Tomatoes, saffron, olive oil and fish hint at the Catalan origin of this savory dish. You can substitute any firm fish, including halibut, salmon or Boston bluefish.

Per serving: about
- 260 calories
- 5 g fat
- high source of fiber
- 19 g protein
- 34 g carbohydrate
- good source of iron

2	potatoes	2
4	carrots	4
1 lb	skinless monkfish fillet	500 g
1/2 tsp	salt	2 mL
1/4 tsp	pepper	1 mL
2 tsp	olive oil	10 mL
2	onions, chopped	2
3	cloves garlic, minced	3
1-1/2 tsp	dried thyme	7 mL
1	bay leaf	1
1-1/2 cups	fish or vegetable stock	375 mL
3/4 cup	dry white wine	175 mL
1/4 tsp	saffron threads	1 mL
1	can (19 oz/540 mL) tomatoes, drained and chopped	1
2 tbsp	finely chopped fresh parsley	25 mL

● Peel potatoes if desired; cut potatoes and carrots into finger-size sticks. Set aside.

● Remove any membrane from fish; cut into 1-inch (2.5 cm) cubes. Sprinkle with half each of the salt and pepper. In large nonstick skillet, heat oil over medium-high heat; cook fish for 4 minutes or until opaque and barely flakes when tested with fork. Transfer to plate.

● Add potatoes, carrots, onions, garlic, thyme, bay leaf and remaining salt and pepper to skillet; cook over medium heat, stirring often, for 4 minutes.

● Stir in stock, wine and saffron; bring to boil. Reduce heat, cover and simmer, stirring occasionally, for about 20 minutes or until vegetables are almost tender. Stir in tomatoes; simmer, uncovered, for about 15 minutes or just until vegetables are tender.

● Return fish to pan; cook for about 2 minutes or until steaming. Discard bay leaf. Serve sprinkled with parsley. Makes 4 servings.

TIPS: ● Instead of white wine, use 1/2 cup (125 mL) fish stock and 2 tbsp (25 mL) white wine vinegar.

● To turn the stew into a soup, add the juice from the tomatoes.

● Saffron is pricier than gold, and a pinch of much less expensive ground turmeric can be substituted for saffron if desired.

Mushroom Vegetable Ribollita

2 tbsp	olive oil	25 mL
2 cups	sliced mushrooms (about 6 oz/175 g)	500 mL
3	cloves garlic, minced	3
2	onions, chopped	2
2	carrots, diced	2
2 cups	chopped cabbage	500 mL
1-1/2 tsp	each dried thyme and marjoram	7 mL
3 cups	vegetable or chicken stock	750 mL
1	can (28 oz/796 mL) tomatoes, chopped	1
1 tbsp	balsamic or red wine vinegar	15 mL
1/4 tsp	pepper	1 mL
Pinch	salt	Pinch
1	can (19 oz/540 mL) white kidney beans, drained and rinsed	1
5 cups	torn fresh spinach	1.25 L
9	slices stale Italian bread	9
1/4 cup	grated Romano cheese	50 mL

● In large saucepan, heat oil over medium heat; cook mushrooms, garlic, onions and carrots, stirring occasionally, for about 8 minutes or until onions are softened.

● Stir in cabbage, thyme and marjoram; cover and cook over low heat, stirring occasionally, for about 10 minutes or until cabbage is softened.

● Stir in stock, tomatoes, vinegar, pepper and salt; bring to boil. Reduce heat and simmer, uncovered, for 20 minutes. Stir in kidney beans and spinach; simmer until spinach is wilted. (Ribollita can be prepared to this point and refrigerated in airtight container for up to 24 hours.)

● Ladle soup into 13- x 9-inch (3 L) glass baking dish. Cut bread into 1-inch (2.5 cm) cubes; arrange evenly over soup. Sprinkle with Romano cheese. Cover and bake in 350°F (180°C) oven for 40 minutes; uncover and bake for about 10 minutes longer or until bubbling and top is crusty and golden. Makes 6 servings.

The Tuscany region of Italy is the home of ribollita, a thick minestrone-type soup traditionally layered and baked with leftover sourdough bread. This version is topped with sourdough croutons that soak up some of the juices and bake up crunchy and golden.

Per serving: about
- 350 calories
- 8 g fat
- very high source of fiber
- excellent source of iron
- 15 g protein
- 56 g carbohydrate
- good source of calcium

SUBSTITUTIONS FOR FRESH OR FROZEN INGREDIENTS

● **Chopped Leeks, Shallots or Green Onions:** Regular cooking onions aren't quite the same but will do the job.

● **Leeks:** Use the green part of green onions, slitting them first before slicing across thinly.

● **Lemon Grass:** Replace with grated lemon rind in a more modest quantity.

● **Cheeses:** Pecorino or Asiago can stand in for Parmesan; Cheddar for Monterey Jack. Most blue cheeses are interchangeable, but note that Danish Blue is stronger than Stilton or Gorgonzola and needs to be tempered with some mild cream cheese. Brie and Camembert are close to each other in flavor.

● **Fresh Coriander or Cilantro:** The best substitute is chopped fresh parsley along with dried cilantro.

● **Fresh Herbs:** Choose crumbled or crushed dried herbs rather than powdered versions. Usually, one-third the amount of dried herbs replaces the flavor of fresh. A sprinkle of fresh parsley brightens most dishes, whatever the dried herb used.

● **Fish Stock:** In most dishes, chicken stock will work. When a strong taste of the sea is required, substitute a modest amount of clam juice.

● **Vegetarian Stock:** When a recipe is completely vegetarian except for chicken stock, you can substitute vegetable stock, either homemade from cooked mild-flavored vegetables or produced from powder.

● **Gingerroot:** There's nothing quite like it, but a quarter of the amount of dried ginger can help.

Easy Gremolata Camembert ▲

Embellished and baked Camembert and Brie cheeses are popular party fare. This lemony garlic- and parsley-topped version is a welcome departure from sweet, nutty ones. Crisp flatbread or melba toast rounds go perfectly with it.

Per serving: about
• 100 calories
• 8 g fat
• 6 g protein
• 1 g carbohydrate

2 tbsp	chopped fresh parsley	25 mL
1	clove garlic, minced	1
1/2 tsp	grated lemon rind	2 mL
1 tsp	lemon juice	5 mL
1	round (4 oz/125 g) Camembert or Brie cheese	1

● In small bowl, combine parsley, garlic, lemon rind and juice; set aside.

● Cut Camembert cheese in half to make 2 discs. Spread parsley mixture over bottom half; top with remaining cheese.

● Place in heatproof serving dish; cover with foil and bake in 375°F (190°C) oven for 10 to 15 minutes or until cheese is softened and starts to melt. Makes 4 servings.

Mushroom Bruschetta

1	piece (6-inch/15 cm) baguette	1
1	clove garlic, halved	1
1 tbsp	butter	15 mL
6 cups	sliced mushrooms (1 lb/500 g)	1.5 L
1/4 cup	chopped green onions	50 mL
1/4 cup	chopped fresh parsley	50 mL
2 tsp	dried basil	10 mL
1/2 cup	freshly grated Parmesan cheese	125 mL

● Slice baguette crosswise into 1/2-inch (1 cm) thick diagonal slices. Place on baking sheet; broil, turning once, for 2 minutes or until golden. Rub tops with cut side of garlic; discard garlic.

● In large nonstick skillet, melt butter over medium-high heat; cook mushrooms, stirring often, for about 8 minutes or until browned and liquid is evaporated.

● Stir in onions, parsley and basil; cook for 1 minute. Spoon over bread; sprinkle with cheese. Broil for about 3 minutes or until cheese is melted. Makes 12 pieces.

Since this grilled rustic bread topped with mushrooms is at its best crisp and bubbling from the oven, why not serve it as guests gather in the kitchen to chat and help put the finishing touches on dinner?

Per piece: about
- 60 calories
- 3 g protein
- 3 g fat
- 6 g carbohydrate

Smoked Trout Spread

8 oz	smoked trout fillets	250 g
1	pkg (4 oz/125 g) light cream cheese, softened	1
3 tbsp	light mayonnaise	50 mL
2 tbsp	chopped fresh dill	25 mL
2 tbsp	lemon juice	25 mL
1 tsp	prepared horseradish	5 mL
1/4 tsp	pepper	1 mL
2 tbsp	toasted chopped walnuts	25 mL
	Fresh dill sprigs	

● In food processor, purée trout, cream cheese, mayonnaise, chopped dill, lemon juice, horseradish and pepper until smooth.

● Spoon into serving bowl. Garnish edge of bowl with walnuts and center with dill sprigs. *(Spread can be covered and refrigerated for up to 8 hours. Let stand at room temperature for 30 minutes before serving.)* Makes about 1-1/2 cups (375 mL).

This tasty, easy-to-prepare spread can be made ahead, ready for guests to enjoy with a variety of vegetables and multigrain crackers.

Per 2 tbsp (25 mL): about
- 70 calories
- 5 g protein
- 5 g fat
- 1 g carbohydrate

Warm Artichoke Parmesan Spread

1	can (14 oz/398 mL) artichoke hearts	1
1 cup	freshly grated Parmesan cheese	250 mL
1/4 cup	light mayonnaise	50 mL
1 tsp	grated lemon rind	5 mL
2 tbsp	lemon juice	25 mL
1	clove garlic, minced	1
Pinch	each cayenne, paprika, salt and black pepper	Pinch

● Drain artichokes, pressing out moisture. Set 1 tbsp (15 mL) of the Parmesan cheese aside.

● In food processor, blend remaining cheese, artichokes, mayonnaise, lemon rind and juice for about 2 minutes or until fairly smooth. Stir in garlic, cayenne, paprika, salt and black pepper.

● Spread in shallow 2-cup (500 mL) ovenproof serving dish; sprinkle with reserved cheese. Bake in 400°F (200°C) oven for about 20 minutes or until edge is golden. Serve warm. Makes about 1-1/3 cups (325 mL).

Even guests who wouldn't tackle a whole artichoke happily dig into this dip.

Per 2 tbsp (25 mL): about
- 75 calories
- 5 g protein
- 5 g fat
- 4 g carbohydrate

Weekend Mornings

Welcome to the weekend, and the first pleasure of the day — a relaxed meal at the table, with time for extra coffee and catching up with the news, family or friends. Whether you choose a delightful brunch frittata or warm-from-the-oven muffins for breakfast, here's how to get your weekend off to a delicious start.

Spring Brunch Frittata ▶

Fiddleheads, available fresh in the spring or frozen all year round, give a satisfying frittata a refreshing new twist. If you gather or buy them fresh, trim off the ends and brush away the tissue-papery brown covering. Like asparagus, they need little cooking — just 3 to 5 minutes in broiling water — and taste best with a squirt of butter or a simple vinaigrette.

Per serving: about
• 235 calories   • 16 g protein
• 16 g fat   • 6 g carbohydrate
• good source
  of calcium

1	pkg (300 g) frozen fiddlehead greens	1
1 tbsp	butter	15 mL
4	large green onions, sliced	4
1	sweet red pepper, thinly sliced	1
12	eggs	12
1-1/2 cups	shredded fontina or mozzarella cheese	375 mL
3/4 cup	fresh bread crumbs	175 mL
1 tsp	salt	5 mL
1/2 tsp	pepper	2 mL

● In pot of boiling water, cook fiddleheads for 2 minutes; drain. In skillet, melt butter over medium heat; cook onions, stirring occasionally, for about 3 minutes or until softened. Add red pepper and fiddleheads; cook, stirring, for 1 minute. Let stand for about 5 minutes or until slightly cooled.

● Meanwhile, in bowl, beat eggs; stir in 1-1/4 cups (300 mL) of the fontina cheese, bread crumbs, salt and pepper.

● Reserve 1 cup (250 mL) of the fiddlehead mixture; scrape remaining mixture into lightly greased 10-inch (25 cm) pie plate. Pour egg mixture over top. Sprinkle with reserved fiddlehead mixture and remaining cheese.

● Bake in 350°F (180°C) oven for 30 to 35 minutes or until puffed and set in center. Let stand for 5 minutes. Makes 8 servings.

FRUIT SALAD

Start breakfast or brunch with a refreshing, juicy fruit salad.
● Holding 2 pink grapefruits, one at a time, over bowl to catch juices, cut off rind and pith. Cut around sections to release from membranes; transfer to serving bowl. Squeeze membranes through sieve set over bowl; transfer juice to serving bowl. Cut 1 cantaloupe in half; scoop out seeds. Cut into wedges; cut off rind. Cut wedges into bite-size pieces; add to bowl. Add 1-1/2 cups (375 mL) green grapes and 1 cup (250 mL) quartered strawberries; toss gently to combine. Garnish with mint. Makes 8 servings.

Per serving: about • 70 calories • 1 g protein • 1 g fat • 17 g carbohydrate

Spring Brunch Frittata and individual Fruit Salads

Smoked Salmon Sandwich Strata

1/3 cup	herbed cream cheese, softened	75 mL
12	slices egg bread	12
2	green onions, minced	2
12	slices smoked salmon (about 5 oz/150 g)	12
4	eggs	4
2 cups	milk	500 mL
2 tsp	Dijon mustard	10 mL
1/4 tsp	each dried dillweed and pepper	1 mL
Pinch	salt	Pinch
1/2 cup	shredded Swiss cheese	125 mL
	Chopped green onions	

● Spread cream cheese evenly over bread. Sprinkle half of the slices with minced onions; top evenly with smoked salmon. Top with remaining bread slices, cheese side down; cut in half diagonally.

● Arrange 3 sandwich halves, cut side down and overlapping slightly, along center of greased 13- x 9-inch (3 L) baking dish. Arrange remaining halves, cut side down, in circle around center layer, overlapping and curving slightly to fit.

● In bowl, whisk together eggs, milk, mustard, dill, pepper and salt; pour over strata. Sprinkle with Swiss cheese. Cover with plastic wrap; refrigerate for at least 4 hours or for up to 12 hours.

● Bake in 350°F (180°C) oven for about 35 minutes or until set and lightly golden. Let stand on rack for 10 minutes. Garnish with chopped onions. Makes 8 servings.

Crusty on top, deliciously tender underneath, this sophisticated strata contains golden sandwiches of herbed cream cheese, smoked salmon and green onions sprinkled with Swiss cheese.

Per serving: about
- 290 calories
- 16 g fat
- good source of calcium
- 14 g protein
- 23 g carbohydrate

Pesto Bruschetta Strata ◄

3 tbsp	pesto sauce	50 mL
16	thin slices Italian bread	16
8	slices Black Forest ham	8
4 oz	mozzarella cheese, thinly sliced	125 g
5	eggs	5
2-1/4 cups	milk	550 mL
1/4 tsp	each dried basil and pepper	1 mL
	TOPPING	
1-1/2 cups	chopped tomatoes	375 mL
1/3 cup	finely chopped green onion	75 mL
1	small clove garlic, minced	1
2 tsp	pesto sauce	10 mL
3 tbsp	freshly grated Parmesan cheese	50 mL

● Spread pesto evenly over 8 slices of the bread; top with ham and cheese slices. Top with remaining bread slices; cut in half. Arrange halves, cut side down and overlapping slightly, to form two circles or ovals in greased 13- x 9-inch (3 L) baking dish.

● Whisk together eggs, milk, basil and pepper; pour over strata. Cover and refrigerate for at least 4 hours or for up to 12 hours. Bake in 350°F (180°C) oven for 35 to 40 minutes or until set and golden.

● TOPPING: Stir together tomatoes, onion, garlic and pesto; sprinkle evenly over strata. Sprinkle with Parmesan cheese. Broil for 2 minutes or until topping is heated through and lightly golden. Let stand on rack for 10 minutes. Makes 8 servings.

This tasty dish has all the makings of a family-pleasing meal — ham, cheese and a crunchy tomato-basil topping.

Per serving: about
- 330 calories
- 13 g fat
- good source of calcium and iron
- 20 g protein
- 32 g carbohydrate

Double Hot Chocolate

Who can resist old-fashioned cocoa? Or, in this case, new-fashioned hot chocolate with a deep, rich, double-chocolate flavor that's perfect for kids and adults alike.

Per serving: about
- 225 calories
- 9 g protein
- 8 g fat
- 32 g carbohydrate
- excellent source of calcium

1 oz	unsweetened chocolate, coarsely chopped	30 g
3 tbsp	granulated sugar	50 mL
2 tbsp	unsweetened cocoa powder	25 mL
1 tsp	instant coffee granules	5 mL
4 cups	milk	1 L
4	marshmallows	4

● In saucepan, whisk together chocolate, sugar, cocoa, coffee granules and 1/4 cup (50 mL) of the milk over medium-low heat until melted and smooth.

● Gradually whisk in remaining milk; heat until steaming. Serve immediately in mugs; top each with marshmallow. Makes 4 servings.

Fruity Granola Yogurt Trifle ▼

Trifle for breakfast? You bet! Especially when it's made with delicious and nutritious ingredients such as homemade granola, yogurt and luscious fresh fruit.

Per serving: about
- 310 calories
- 9 g protein
- 11 g fat
- 47 g carbohydrate
- high source of fiber
- good source of calcium

2 tsp	granulated sugar (optional)	10 mL
3 cups	plain yogurt	750 mL
4 cups	mixed fruit (grapes, sliced kiwifruit and banana, raspberries and/or orange segments)	1 L
	GRANOLA	
1-1/4 cups	rolled oats	300 mL
1/3 cup	shredded coconut	75 mL
1/4 cup	wheat germ	50 mL
1/4 cup	wheat flakes	50 mL

2 tbsp	sliced almonds	25 mL
2 tbsp	unsalted sunflower seeds	25 mL
1/4 cup	liquid honey	50 mL
2 tbsp	vegetable oil	25 mL
1/3 cup	dried cranberries or raisins	75 mL

● GRANOLA: In bowl, stir together rolled oats, coconut, wheat germ, wheat flakes, almonds and sunflower seeds.

● In small saucepan, heat honey with oil over medium-low heat; gradually pour over oat mixture, stirring to coat well. Spread on rimmed baking sheet; bake in 350°F (180°C) oven, stirring frequently, for 10 to 15 minutes or until golden brown.

● Transfer pan to rack; stir in cranberries. Let cool, stirring occasionally to prevent clumping. (Granola can be refrigerated in airtight container for up to 1 month.)

● Spoon into attractive 6- to 8-cup (1.5 to 2 L) trifle bowl. Stir sugar (if using) into yogurt; pour over granola. (Trifle can be prepared to this point, covered and refrigerated for up to 1 hour.)

● To serve, spoon mixed fruit over yogurt. Makes 8 servings.

Golden Cheese and Onion Loaf

1 tsp	granulated sugar	5 mL
1/2 cup	warm water	125 mL
1-1/2 tsp	quick-rising (instant) dry yeast	7 mL
1/4 cup	milk	50 mL
1/4 cup	plain yogurt	50 mL
2-1/2 cups	all-purpose flour	625 mL
1 tsp	salt	5 mL
	FILLING	
1 tbsp	olive oil	15 mL
1/3 cup	cubed Black Forest ham (2 oz/50 g)	75 mL
2 tsp	butter	10 mL
3 cups	thinly sliced onions	750 mL
1-1/2 tsp	cider vinegar	7 mL
2/3 cup	shredded Cheddar cheese	150 mL
	GLAZE	
1	egg	1
1/4 cup	water	50 mL

● In bowl, dissolve sugar in warm water. Sprinkle in yeast; let stand for 10 minutes or until frothy. Stir in milk and yogurt.

● In large bowl, stir together 1-1/2 cups (375 mL) of the flour and salt. Pour in yeast mixture; stir vigorously with wooden spoon for 3 minutes. Stir in remaining flour until dough comes away from side of bowl.

● Turn out dough onto lightly floured surface. Knead for about 5 minutes or until smooth and elastic. Place in lightly greased bowl, turning to grease all over. Cover with plastic wrap; let rise in warm, draft-free spot until doubled in bulk, about 1-1/2 hours.

● FILLING: Meanwhile, in large skillet, heat 1 tsp (5 mL) of the oil over medium-high heat; cook ham for 2 minutes or until golden at edges and beginning to crisp. Transfer to bowl.

● Add remaining oil and butter to skillet; cook onions over low heat, stirring occasionally, for 20 to 25 minutes or until golden and sweet. Add vinegar; cook for 5 minutes. Stir into ham in bowl; let cool to room temperature.

● Punch down dough; divide in half. Roll or press out one piece into 10- x 6-inch (25 x 15 cm) rectangle. With long side horizontal, spread with half of the filling, leaving 1/2-inch (1 cm) border uncovered at sides and bottom. Sprinkle filling with 1/3 cup (75 mL) of the Cheddar cheese. Starting at top, roll dough firmly into cylinder; press seam tightly to seal. Fold in ends to meet seam; press to seal.

● Place loaf, seam side down, on half of lightly greased baking sheet; cover with tea towel. Repeat with remaining dough, filling and cheese. Place on other half of baking sheet. Let rise until doubled in bulk, about 1 hour.

● GLAZE: Whisk egg with water; brush over loaves. With serrated knife, make shallow slash lengthwise down center of each loaf, being careful not to cut into filling. Bake in 400°F (200°C) oven for 20 minutes or until golden brown and loaves sound hollow when tapped on bottom. Serve warm or let cool on rack. *(Loaves can be refrigerated in plastic bags for up to 1 day.)* Makes 2 small loaves, about 8 slices each.

A *golden swirl of Cheddar, ham and caramelized onions turns a plain loaf into a spectacular addition to a celebratory brunch or buffet.*

Per slice: about
- 105 calories
- 3 g fat
- 4 g protein
- 15 g carbohydrate

BREAD MACHINE METHOD

To make dough only, increase flour to 3 cups (750 mL). In order, place in pan: water, milk, yogurt, salt, sugar and flour. Sprinkle yeast over top, making sure yeast does not touch liquid mixture. According to manufacturer's instructions, choose dough-only setting. Follow instructions above for shaping, filling and baking.

Cheese Blintzes ▼

Old-world blintzes (crêpes wrapped around a cottage-cheese filling) start any day with flair. Serve with fresh fruit or blueberry or strawberry sauce.

Per blintz: about
- 110 calories
- 8 g protein
- 4 g fat
- 9 g carbohydrate

TIP: Blintz wrappers can be stacked between waxed paper, wrapped in plastic wrap and frozen for up to 2 months.

3	eggs	3
1/2 tsp	salt	2 mL
1-1/4 cups	all-purpose flour	300 mL
1/4 cup	butter, melted	50 mL
	FILLING	
1 lb	pressed cottage cheese, softened	500 g
1	egg	1
2 tsp	granulated sugar	10 mL
3/4 tsp	vanilla	4 mL
1/2 tsp	cinnamon	2 mL
Pinch	salt	Pinch

● In blender, combine eggs, salt and 1-1/2 cups (375 mL) water; blend in flour until smooth. Transfer to bowl; cover with plastic wrap. Refrigerate for 1 hour.

● Heat 7-inch (18 cm) crêpe pan over medium-high heat; brush with a little of the butter. Stir batter; pour 3 tbsp (50 mL) into pan, tilting to spread thinly. Cook for 45 to 60 seconds or until set and no moisture remains in center. Invert onto tea towel. Repeat with remaining batter, using up to 2 tbsp (25 mL) of the butter.

● FILLING: In bowl, beat cottage cheese until fluffy; beat in egg, sugar, vanilla, cinnamon and salt. Spoon heaping tablespoonful (15 mL) onto center of light side of each blintz; fold 1 side over filling. Fold over opposite side, then top and bottom, to enclose filling.

● In skillet, heat 2 tsp (10 mL) of the remaining butter over medium heat; cook blintzes, in batches and using remaining butter, for 2 minutes per side or until golden and warmed through. Makes 16 blintzes.

Carrot Apricot Muffin Squares

1	egg	1
1 cup	buttermilk	250 mL
1/3 cup	vegetable oil	75 mL
1 tsp	vanilla	5 mL
2 cups	grated carrots	500 mL
3/4 cup	100% Bran or All-Bran cereal	175 mL
1-1/2 cups	all-purpose flour	375 mL
2/3 cup	finely chopped dried apricots	150 mL
1/2 cup	packed brown sugar	125 mL
1/4 cup	shredded coconut	50 mL
1 tbsp	coarsely grated orange rind	15 mL
1 tsp	each baking powder and baking soda	5 mL
1/2 tsp	salt	2 mL

● In bowl, whisk together egg, buttermilk, oil and vanilla; stir in carrots and cereal. Let stand for 5 minutes.

● Meanwhile, in large bowl, stir together flour, apricots, sugar, coconut, orange rind, baking powder, baking soda and salt. Pour carrot mixture over dry ingredients; stir just until moistened.

● Spread in greased 9-inch (2.5 L) square cake pan. Bake in 375°F (190°C) oven for about 40 minutes or until center springs back when gently touched. Let cool on rack. Cut into squares. Makes 16 squares.

Have a dose of goodness along with a good-morning dash of taste as you nibble on these muffin squares. Carrots and apricots are rich in beta-carotene, and bran cereal delivers fiber.

Per square: about
- 155 calories
- 3 g protein
- 6 g fat
- 25 g carbohydrate

Honey Bran Muffins

2	eggs	2
1-1/3 cups	buttermilk	325 mL
1/3 cup	vegetable oil	75 mL
1/4 cup	liquid honey	50 mL
2 tsp	vanilla	10 mL
1-1/2 cups	100% Bran or All-Bran cereal	375 mL
1-1/2 cups	raisins	375 mL
1-3/4 cups	all-purpose flour	425 mL
1/2 cup	packed brown sugar	125 mL
1-1/2 tsp	baking soda	7 mL
1/2 tsp	each cinnamon and salt	2 mL

● In bowl, whisk together eggs, buttermilk, oil, honey and vanilla; stir in cereal and raisins. Let stand for 5 minutes.

● Meanwhile, in separate bowl, stir together flour, sugar, baking soda, cinnamon and salt. Pour bran mixture over dry ingredients; stir just until moistened. Spoon into greased or paper-lined muffin cups, filling to top.

● Bake in 375°F (190°C) oven for about 25 minutes or until golden and tops are firm to the touch. Let cool in pan for 5 minutes; transfer to rack and let cool completely. Makes 12 muffins.

VARIATIONS
● MUFFIN TOPS: Spoon about 1/3 cup (75 mL) batter into greased muffin top pans, spreading slightly. Bake for about 10 minutes or until golden and firm to the touch. (Muffin tops will be moist and slightly flat.) Makes about 18 muffin tops.

● MINI MUFFINS: Spoon scant 1/4 cup (50 mL) batter into greased mini muffin pans. Bake for 10 to 12 minutes or until golden and tops are springy to the touch. Makes about 14 mini muffins.

When using honey to sweeten muffins, choose one with a strong flavor — buckwheat is ideal. Then you can really taste the honey.

Per muffin: about
- 285 calories
- 6 g protein
- 8 g fat
- 53 g carbohydrate
- high source of fiber
- good source of iron

Raspberry Lemon Muffins

When fresh raspberries are not available, use individually quick-frozen ones or dried fruit such as cranberries, cherries, blueberries, slivered apricots or golden raisins.

Per muffin: about
- 235 calories
- 9 fat
- 4 protein
- 35 carbohydrate

2 cups	all-purpose flour	500 mL
1/2 cup	granulated sugar	125 mL
1 tbsp	baking powder	15 mL
1/2 tsp	salt	2 mL
1 cup	raspberries	250 mL
1 tbsp	coarsely grated lemon rind	15 mL
1	egg	1
1 cup	milk	250 mL
1/3 cup	vegetable oil	75 mL
1/4 cup	lemon juice	50 mL
	TOPPING	
1/4 cup	icing sugar	50 mL
1 tsp	lemon juice	5 mL

● In large bowl, stir together flour, sugar, baking powder and salt; add raspberries and lemon rind, tossing to combine.

● Whisk together egg, milk, oil and lemon juice; pour over dry ingredients and stir just until moistened.

● Spoon into greased or paper-lined muffin cups, filling to top. Bake in 375°F (190°C) oven for about 25 minutes or until golden and tops are firm to the touch. Let cool in pan for 5 minutes; transfer to rack and let cool completely.

● TOPPING: Stir icing sugar with lemon juice; drizzle over muffins. Makes 10 muffins.

Gone-to-Seed Muffins

This recipe proves that muffins are more than cupcakes with good PR. Bran, some whole wheat flour, flax seeds and dates pack nutrition into these pleasing, fine-textured muffins.

Per muffin: about
- 265 calories
- 9 g fat
- 6 g protein
- 42 g carbohydrate

1-3/4 cups	all-purpose flour	425 mL
1/2 cup	whole wheat flour	125 mL
1/2 cup	packed brown sugar	125 mL
1/4 cup	natural wheat bran	50 mL
2 tbsp	each flax seeds, poppy seeds and sesame seeds	25 mL
2 tsp	baking powder	10 mL
1 tsp	baking soda	5 mL
1/2 tsp	salt	2 mL
1 cup	chopped dates	250 mL
2 tbsp	coarsely grated orange rind	25 mL
1	egg	1
1-1/2 cups	buttermilk	375 mL
1/3 cup	vegetable oil	75 mL
1/4 cup	orange juice	50 mL

● In large bowl, stir together all-purpose and whole wheat flours, brown sugar, bran, flax, poppy and sesame seeds, baking powder, baking soda and salt. Sprinkle with dates and orange rind.

● Whisk together egg, buttermilk, oil and orange juice; pour over dry ingredients and stir just until moistened. Spoon into greased or paper-lined muffin cups, filling to top.

● Bake in 375°F (190°C) oven for 20 to 25 minutes or until golden and tops are firm to the touch. Let cool in pan for 5 minutes; transfer to rack and let cool completely. Makes 12 muffins.

MUFFIN-MAKING BASICS

● Grease muffin cups with shortening and a pastry brush, spray with vegetable oil or line with paper liners (available in supermarkets).

● When the batter does not fill all the muffin cups in a pan, pour about 1 inch (2.5 cm) water into empty cups to prevent them from burning.

● Let baked muffins cool in pan for about 5 minutes. This allows the still-hot and delicate structure to firm up before being transferred to racks.

● Run a blunt knife around edge of cooled muffins to loosen before lifting out of pan.

Spiced Apple Coffee Cake ▲

3/4 cup	butter, softened	175 mL
3/4 cup	granulated sugar	175 mL
3/4 cup	packed brown sugar	175 mL
3	eggs	3
1 tsp	vanilla	5 mL
2-2/3 cups	all-purpose flour	650 mL
1-1/2 tsp	baking powder	7 mL
1-1/2 tsp	baking soda	7 mL
1/2 tsp	each cinnamon and salt	2 mL
2 cups	sour cream or plain yogurt	500 mL
	FILLING	
2	large tart apples	2
1/3 cup	packed brown sugar	75 mL
2 tsp	cinnamon	10 mL
1/2 cup	chopped pecans	125 mL

● FILLING: Peel, core and quarter apples. Slice 4 of the quarters; place in bowl. Chop remaining quarters; place in separate bowl. Toss each with half each of the brown sugar and cinnamon.

● In large bowl, beat together butter, granulated sugar and brown sugar until combined; beat in eggs, one at a time, beating well after each addition. Beat in vanilla.

● Combine flour, baking powder, baking soda, cinnamon and salt; using wooden spoon, stir into butter mixture alternately with sour cream, making 3 additions of flour and 2 of sour cream.

● Arrange apple slices in overlapping circle in ungreased 10-inch (3 L) Bundt pan. Scrape half of the batter over top. Sprinkle with chopped apples, then pecans. Spread with remaining batter.

● Bake in 350°F (180°C) oven for 55 to 65 minutes or until top is golden and cake tester inserted in center comes out clean. Let cool in pan on rack for 20 minutes. Invert onto cake plate and serve warm. Makes 12 servings.

T*he irresistible aroma of sweet spices, butter, sugar and apples baking in the oven will get even the worst of the sleepyheads out of bed quickly.*

Per serving: about
- 460 calories
- 22 g fat
- good source of iron
- 6 g protein
- 61 g carbohydrate

For the Love of Cooking

This chapter is for all of us who love to cook and to explore new tastes and cuisines. Thank goodness for the weekend — with time to search out exotic ingredients, perfect culinary techniques or simply to linger over the preparation and presentation of special dishes.

Coconut Curry Shrimp ▶

Served over basmati rice and garnished with julienned carrots, cucumber slices and chopped red pepper, this dish is one invitation to the world of fine tastes you won't turn down.

Per serving: about
- 530 calories
- 26 g protein
- 21 g fat
- 60 g carbohydrate
- excellent source of iron

TIP: Coconut milk is available in cans or powdered form at Asian food shops and some grocery stores. Do not confuse sweetened cream of coconut, used mainly for desserts, with unsweetened coconut milk.

1 cup	chopped onion	250 mL
3/4 cup	chopped sweet red pepper	175 mL
2 tbsp	chopped gingerroot	25 mL
3	cloves garlic	3
1 tsp	grated lime rind	5 mL
1/2 tsp	hot pepper flakes	2 mL
2 tbsp	ground almonds	25 mL
2 tsp	ground coriander	10 mL
3/4 tsp	paprika	4 mL
1/4 tsp	turmeric	1 mL
1-1/2 tsp	black or brown mustard seeds	7 mL
1 tbsp	vegetable oil	15 mL
1-1/4 tsp	salt	6 mL
1 cup	coconut milk	250 mL
1 tbsp	lime juice	15 mL
1 lb	shrimp, peeled and deveined	500 g
2 tbsp	toasted sliced almonds	25 mL
1 tbsp	chopped fresh coriander	15 mL

● In blender or food processor, chop together onion, red pepper, ginger, garlic, lime rind and hot pepper flakes. Scrape down side of bowl. Add ground almonds, coriander, paprika and turmeric; blend to form paste.

● In large nonstick skillet, toast mustard seeds over medium-high heat, shaking pan constantly, for 3 minutes or until seeds turn grey and pop. Remove from pan and set aside.

● Reduce heat to medium. Add oil to skillet, swirling to coat; cook reserved paste, stirring with flat wooden spatula and scraping bottom of pan, for 12 minutes or until deep orange and separated into dry clumps.

● Return mustard seeds to pan. Add 1 cup (250 mL) water and 3/4 tsp (4 mL) of the salt; bring to boil. Reduce heat and simmer for 5 minutes. Strain through fine sieve into bowl, pressing to extract liquid.

● Wipe skillet clean. Return strained liquid to skillet. Gently whisk in coconut milk and lime juice until blended; bring to boil. Reduce heat and add shrimp; simmer gently, stirring occasionally, for about 3 minutes or just until shrimp are pink.

● To serve, spoon curry over basmati rice. Sprinkle with almonds and fresh coriander. Makes 4 servings.

Halibut Package with Dill Pesto ▲

Baking fish en papillote adds excitement to a meal as the parchment paper package arrives at the table crackling and puffed with fragrant steam.

Per serving: about
- 220 calories
- 12 g fat
- 25 g protein
- 3 g carbohydrate

1/3 cup	each loosely packed fresh dill and parsley	75 mL
1/3 cup	chopped green onions or chives	75 mL
1/3 cup	toasted sliced almonds	75 mL
1/4 cup	olive oil	50 mL
1	clove garlic, chopped	1
1/2 tsp	salt	2 mL
1/4 tsp	pepper	1 mL
8	halibut fillets or steaks (4 oz/125 g each)	8
1	large roasted sweet red pepper, cut in 8 strips	1

● In blender or food processor, chop together dill, parsley, onions, almonds, oil, garlic, salt and pepper until almost puréed.

● Line baking sheet with parchment paper or foil. Pat fish dry; place in single layer on one-half of paper. Spread each piece with 1 tbsp (15 mL) of the dill mixture. Top with red pepper strip. Fold remaining half of paper over fish, crimping edges to seal.

● Bake in 425°F (220°C) oven for about 10 minutes or until fish is opaque and flakes easily when tested with fork. Makes 8 servings.

Chunky Fish Chowder Stew

1	leek	1
1	small bulb fennel	1
1	large sweet potato	1
1 lb	halibut or cod	500 g
1 tbsp	olive oil	15 mL
2 oz	back bacon, diced	60 g
1	onion, coarsely chopped	1
2	cloves garlic, minced	2
1	can (28 oz/796 mL) tomatoes, puréed	1
1 cup	dry white wine or water	250 mL
1/2 tsp	each salt and pepper	2 mL
8 oz	shrimp, peeled and deveined	250 g
1/4 cup	chopped fresh parsley	50 mL

● Trim leek and fennel; cut into 1-inch (2.5 cm) chunks. Peel potato; cut into 1-inch (2.5 cm) chunks. Cut halibut into 2-inch (5 cm) chunks. Set all aside separately.

● In Dutch oven, heat oil over medium-high heat; cook bacon for 5 minutes. Add leek, onion and garlic; reduce heat to medium-low and cook, stirring, for 8 minutes. Add fennel, tomatoes and wine; bring to boil. Add sweet potato; reduce heat, cover and simmer for about 20 minutes or until tender. Season with salt and pepper.

● Add halibut and shrimp; bring to boil. Reduce heat, cover and simmer for 5 minutes or until fish is opaque and shrimp pink. Serve sprinkled with parsley. Makes 6 servings.

This fine halibut-and-shrimp stew is aromatic with fennel and garlic, and simply gorgeous with chunks of sweet potato.

Per serving: about
- 225 calories
- 4 g fat
- good source of iron
- 24 g protein
- 21 g carbohydrate

Warm Couscous with Roasted Fall Vegetables

4 cups	coarsely cubed peeled butternut squash or sweet potato	1 L
1	red onion, chopped	1
2	cloves garlic, quartered	2
2 tbsp	olive oil	25 mL
1 cup	cooked chick-peas or kidney beans	250 mL
1/2 cup	diced sweet red pepper	125 mL
1-1/2 cups	vegetable stock or water	375 mL
1 tsp	ground cumin	5 mL
1 cup	couscous	250 mL
1/2 cup	frozen green peas, thawed	125 mL
1/4 cup	white wine vinegar	50 mL
1/4 cup	vegetable oil	50 mL
1 tsp	dried oregano	5 mL
3/4 tsp	salt	4 mL
Pinch	cayenne pepper	Pinch
1/2 cup	chopped fresh coriander or parsley	125 mL

● In 13- x 9-inch (3 L) baking dish, toss together squash, onion, garlic and oil; roast in 400°F (200°C) oven, stirring once, for 20 to 30 minutes or until vegetables are browned on edges and just tender. Transfer to large bowl; add chick-peas and red pepper.

● Meanwhile, in saucepan, bring stock and cumin to boil; stir in couscous and peas. Remove from heat; cover and let stand for 5 minutes. Fluff with fork.

● Sprinkle couscous over squash mixture. Sprinkle with vinegar, oil, oregano, salt and cayenne; toss gently. *(Recipe can be prepared to this point, covered and refrigerated for up to 1 day.)* Toss with coriander. Makes 6 servings.

Celebrate the fall harvest of healthy beta-carotene- and fiber-rich vegetables with this delicious vegetarian main course. It can be served warm or at room temperature.

Per serving: about
- 380 calories
- 15 g fat
- very high source of fiber
- 10 g protein
- 54 g carbohydrate
- good source of iron

Salmon Strudels ▶

Golden phyllo packages of succulent salmon nestled on a bed of fresh spinach and rice make a spectacular dinner entrée. Pair with lighter fare — a soup such as consommé or gazpacho to start, fresh mesclun (see p. 61) and green vegetables alongside — and fruit sorbet to finish.

Per serving (Salmon Strudels): about
- 650 calories
- 29 g fat
- good source of calcium
- excellent source of fiber
- 42 g protein
- 55 g carbohydrate
- excellent source of iron

Per serving (Wine Butter Sauce): about
- 285 calories
- 31 g fat
- 1 g protein
- 2 g carbohydrate

2	pkg (10 oz/284 g each) fresh spinach	2
1 tsp	lemon juice	5 mL
Pinch	nutmeg	Pinch
1	salmon fillet (1-1/2 lb/750 g)	1
8	sheets phyllo pastry	8
1/3 cup	butter, melted	75 mL
	Wine Butter Sauce (optional), recipe follows	
	RICE	
2 tsp	butter	10 mL
1	onion, chopped	1
3/4 cup	sliced mushrooms	175 mL
3/4 cup	vegetable stock	175 mL
2/3 cup	water	150 mL
1/4 tsp	salt	1 mL
Pinch	pepper	Pinch
1/4 cup	wild rice, rinsed	50 mL
1/3 cup	long-grain rice	75 mL

● RICE: In saucepan, melt butter over medium heat; cook onion and mushrooms, stirring occasionally, for 5 minutes or until softened. Add stock, water, salt and pepper; bring to boil. Add wild rice; return to boil. Reduce heat, cover and simmer for 35 minutes. Stir in long-grain rice; simmer, covered, for 25 minutes or just until liquid is absorbed and rice is tender. Let cool.

● Trim and rinse spinach; shake off excess water. In large saucepan, cook spinach, covered and with just the water clinging to leaves, over medium heat for 8 minutes or until wilted. Drain in sieve, pressing out moisture. Chop and toss with lemon juice and nutmeg. Set aside.

● Cut salmon crosswise into 4 pieces; slide knife between skin and flesh to remove skin.

● Lay 1 sheet of phyllo on work surface, keeping remaining phyllo covered with damp cloth to prevent drying out. Brush with about 2 tsp (10 mL) of the butter. Place second sheet on top; brush with butter.

● About 1 inch (2.5 cm) from one long side of pastry, spoon 1/2 cup (125 mL) rice mixture lengthwise into 3-inch (8 cm) wide strip. Arrange one-quarter of the spinach over rice. Top with 1 piece of salmon. Fold 1-inch (2.5 cm) border over filling; fold each side over and roll up.

● Place strudels, seam side down, on greased baking sheet. Brush with butter. Repeat with remaining ingredients to form 4 packages. Bake in 425°F (220°C) oven for 15 to 20 minutes or until golden. Serve with Wine Butter Sauce (if using). Makes 4 servings.

WINE BUTTER SAUCE		
1/4 cup	white wine vinegar	50 mL
1/4 cup	white wine	50 mL
2 tbsp	finely minced shallots or onion	25 mL
1/4 tsp	each salt and pepper	1 mL
2/3 cup	unsalted butter, cut into 1/2-inch (1 cm) cubes	150 mL
1 tbsp	chopped fresh parsley	15 mL

● In saucepan, bring vinegar, wine, shallots, salt and pepper to boil; boil for 5 minutes or until reduced to 2 tbsp (25 mL). Reduce heat to low; vigorously whisk in butter, a few cubes at a time, until thickened and smooth. Stir in parsley. Makes 3/4 cup (175 mL), enough for 4 servings.

Chicken with Corn-and-Pepper Salsa ◄

1/2 cup	oil-and-vinegar salad dressing	125 mL
1 tbsp	grated lime rind	15 mL
3 tbsp	lime juice	50 mL
1 tsp	chili powder	5 mL
1/2 tsp	salt	2 mL
1/4 tsp	pepper	1 mL
1	clove garlic, minced	1
6	boneless skinless chicken breasts (about 2 lb/1 kg total)	6
	CORN-AND-PEPPER SALSA	
1	can (10 oz/284 mL) corn kernels, drained	1
1	jar (12 oz/340 g) roasted sweet red peppers, drained and coarsely chopped	1
1/4 cup	oil-and-vinegar salad dressing	50 mL
2 tbsp	finely chopped fresh coriander or parsley	25 mL
1 tbsp	grated lime rind	15 mL
3 tbsp	lime juice	50 mL
1 tsp	finely chopped jalapeño pepper	5 mL

● In glass bowl, combine salad dressing, lime rind and juice, chili powder, salt, pepper and garlic; add chicken, turning to coat. Cover and marinate in refrigerator for at least 2 hours or for up to 3 hours, turning once.

● CORN-AND-PEPPER SALSA: Meanwhile, in bowl, combine corn, red peppers, salad dressing, coriander, lime rind and juice, and jalapeño pepper; cover and refrigerate until chilled or for up to 3 hours.

● Reserving marinade, place chicken on greased grill over medium-high heat, or on top rack of broiler; cook, turning twice and brushing with marinade, for 10 to 15 minutes or until no longer pink inside. Serve with Corn-and-Pepper Salsa. Makes 6 servings.

Every year, Canadian Living joins with Newman's Own, Inc., for a recipe contest that raises money for Breakfast for Learning, Canadian Living's foundation for breakfast programs across Canada, as well as for the winner's charity of choice. The prizewinning recipe for 1995, by Louise Blake of Thunder Bay, Ontario, was the inspiration for this memorable dish.

Per serving: about
- 315 calories
- 29 g protein
- 16 g fat
- 16 g carbohydrate

On the Twenty Squash Risotto

1 tbsp	olive oil	15 mL
3 cups	diced seeded peeled squash	750 mL
1	onion, chopped	1
1-1/2 cups	Arborio rice	375 mL
1 cup	Chardonnay wine, warmed	250 mL
3-1/2 cups	(approx) chicken stock, warmed	875 mL
1/4 cup	freshly grated Parmesan cheese	50 mL
1-1/2 tsp	lemon juice	7 mL
	Salt and pepper	

● In large heavy saucepan, heat oil over medium heat; cook squash and onion, stirring occasionally, for 5 minutes or until onion is softened.

● Stir in rice, 1/2 cup (125 mL) of the wine and 1 cup (250 mL) of the stock; bring to boil. Reduce heat and simmer, stirring, for 5 minutes.

● Add remaining wine and 1-1/2 cups (375 mL) stock; simmer, stirring occasionally, for 10 to 15 minutes or until creamy, rice is still slightly firm and squash is tender, adding remaining stock if needed.

● Stir in Parmesan cheese, lemon juice, and salt and pepper to taste. Makes 6 servings.

This golden risotto comes from the kitchen of chef Michael Olson of On the Twenty restaurant in Jordon, Ontario, in the heart of Niagara Peninsula wine country.

Per serving: about
- 285 calories
- 9 g protein
- 5 g fat
- 50 g carbohydrate

Celebration Vegetarian Lasagna ▼

Monica Becker of Winnipeg, Manitoba, was the grand-prize winner in the 1994 Newman's Own, Inc., contest to raise money for Breakfast for Learning and the winner's own charity. We've adapted her spectacular entertaining dish, using regular spaghetti sauce.

Per serving: about
- 525 calories
- 32 g fat
- high source of fiber
- 20 g protein
- 41 g carbohydrate
- excellent source of calcium and iron

1	pkg (10 oz/284 g) fresh spinach	1
3 tbsp	olive oil	50 mL
3	shiitake mushrooms, finely chopped	3
1	portobello mushroom (about 4 oz/125 g), finely chopped	1
1	large shallot or small onion, finely chopped	1
1	jar (700 mL) spaghetti sauce	1
1	jar (6 oz/170 mL) marinated artichoke hearts, drained and chopped	1
1-1/2 tsp	pepper	7 mL
8 oz	spinach lasagna noodles	250 g
8 oz	bocconcini or mozzarella cheese, sliced	250 g
8 oz	mascarpone or ricotta cheese	250 g
1 cup	freshly grated Parmesan cheese	250 mL

● Trim and rinse spinach; shake off excess water. In saucepan, cook spinach, covered and with just the water clinging to leaves, over medium-high heat for about 5 minutes or until wilted. Drain in sieve, reserving cooking water. Press out excess moisture from spinach; chop coarsely and set aside.

● In large saucepan, heat oil over medium-high heat; cook shiitake and portobello mushrooms and shallot, stirring often, for 5 minutes.

● Stir in spaghetti sauce, artichoke hearts, spinach and pepper. Add enough water to reserved cooking water to make 2/3 cup (150 mL); stir into spaghetti sauce. Bring to boil; reduce heat and simmer for 30 minutes.

● Meanwhile, in large pot of boiling salted water, cook noodles for about 8 minutes or until tender but firm. Drain on tea towels.

● Spread about 1 cup (250 mL) of the sauce in 13- x 9-inch (3 L) baking dish. Cover with one-quarter of the noodles, then one-quarter of the sauce. Top with one-third of the bocconcini cheese, then one-third of the mascarpone cheese, then 1/4 cup (50 mL) of the Parmesan cheese. Repeat layers twice.

● Arrange remaining noodles over top; spread with remaining sauce and sprinkle with remaining Parmesan cheese. Bake in 350°F (180°C) oven for 30 to 35 minutes or until bubbly. Let stand for 5 minutes before cutting. Makes 8 servings.

MAKE-YOUR-OWN MESCLUN

Mesclun, originally from France's Provence district, is a flavorful mix of young greens that range in taste from sweet to bitter. To create your own potpourri of tender greens, include some of these popular varieties:

- **Arugula:** soft indented leaves on a central stalk; surprisingly peppery kick.
- **Baby Beet Leaves:** striking red vein accenting the green; fresh in the mouth.
- **Baby Spinach:** deep green; soft, mild and toothsome.
- **Frisée:** belongs to chicory family; pale-green-and-white curly leaves; delicate, chewy texture; mildly bitter.
- **Mâche:** also called lamb's lettuce; tight clusters with small, elongated leaves; subtle hazelnut flavor.
- **Mizuna:** pretty spiked leaves; mustardy sour taste.
- **Radicchio:** leaves are magenta and cream; slightly bitter.
- **Red Oak-Leaf Lettuce:** resembles its name; soft crunch.
- **Tatsoi:** dark green; small, fat, oval shape; meaty, slightly spicy flavor.

Curried Lentil, Wild Rice and Orzo Salad

1/2 cup	wild rice, rinsed	125 mL
2/3 cup	green or brown lentils	150 mL
1/2 cup	orzo pasta	125 mL
1/2 cup	currants	125 mL
1/4 cup	finely chopped red onion	50 mL
1/3 cup	slivered almonds, toasted	75 mL
	DRESSING	
1/4 cup	white wine vinegar	50 mL
1 tsp	ground cumin	5 mL
1 tsp	Dijon mustard	5 mL
1/2 tsp	each granulated sugar, salt and ground coriander	2 mL
1/4 tsp	each turmeric and paprika	1 mL
1/4 tsp	each ground cardamom and nutmeg	1 mL
Pinch	each cinnamon, cloves and cayenne	Pinch
1/3 cup	vegetable oil	75 mL

● In large pot of boiling salted water, cover and cook wild rice for 10 minutes. Add lentils; boil for 20 minutes. Add orzo; boil for about 5 minutes or just until tender. Drain well and transfer to large bowl. Add currants and onion; set aside.

● DRESSING: In small bowl, whisk together vinegar, cumin, mustard, sugar, salt, coriander, turmeric, paprika, cardamom, nutmeg, cinnamon, cloves and cayenne; whisk in oil. Pour over rice mixture and toss gently.

● Let salad cool completely; cover and refrigerate for at least 4 hours or for up to 2 days. Serve sprinkled with almonds. Makes 6 servings.

O*rzo pasta, dark wild rice and firm lentils, plus a slightly sweet-and-tangy curry dressing, make this salad a grand candidate for buffets, potlucks and picnics.*

Per serving: about
- 365 calories
- 17 g fat
- high source of fiber
- 11 g protein
- 45 g carbohydrate
- excellent source of iron

Grilled Bread Salad

Chunky croutons add substance and new appeal to a big bowl of summer greens. Crusty sourdough bread makes croutons that stay crisp even when dressed.

Per serving: about
- 320 calories
- 4 g protein
- 25 g fat
- 25 g carbohydrate

2 tbsp	olive oil	25 mL
1	clove garlic, minced	1
1/4 tsp	each salt and pepper	1 mL
3	slices Italian bread, 3/4 inch (2 cm) thick	3
6 cups	torn romaine lettuce	1.5 L
1	tomato, chopped	1
1	carrot, shredded	1
	VINAIGRETTE	
3 tbsp	white wine vinegar	50 mL
1 tbsp	chopped fresh oregano (or 1 tsp/5 mL dried)	15 mL
1/2 tsp	granulated sugar	2 mL
1/2 tsp	Dijon mustard	2 mL
1/4 tsp	each salt and pepper	1 mL
1	clove garlic, minced	1
1/3 cup	olive oil	75 mL

● Stir together oil, garlic, salt and pepper; brush onto both sides of bread slices. Place on greased grill over medium heat; close lid and cook, turning once, for about 6 minutes or until crisp and golden. Cut into bite-size cubes.

● VINAIGRETTE: In small bowl, whisk together vinegar, oregano, sugar, mustard, salt, pepper and garlic; gradually whisk in oil.

● In salad bowl, combine lettuce, tomato and carrot. Sprinkle with vinaigrette and bread cubes; toss to combine. Makes 4 servings.

Grilled Portobello Mushrooms

Giant portobello mushrooms are a terrific side dish with fish, steak or chops. For a touch of drama, slice thinly on the diagonal and fan over a warmed plate.

Per serving: about
- 165 calories
- 4 g protein
- 16 g fat
- 3 g carbohydrate

4	portobello mushrooms	4
1/4 cup	olive oil	50 mL
3 tbsp	balsamic vinegar	50 mL
2 tsp	chopped fresh thyme (or 1/2 tsp/2 mL dried)	10 mL
Pinch	each salt and pepper	Pinch
1 oz	Parmesan cheese, shaved	30 g

● Remove thick end of mushroom stem, leaving about 1/2 inch (1 cm) attached to cap. Place, smooth side up, in large shallow glass dish.

● Combine oil, vinegar, thyme, salt and pepper; pour over mushrooms, turning and brushing to coat evenly. Let stand for 15 minutes.

● Reserving marinade, place mushrooms, smooth side down, on greased grill over medium-high heat; close lid and cook for 5 minutes. Turn and baste with marinade; cook, covered, for about 3 minutes or until mushrooms yield to the touch when pressed. Arrange Parmesan over top; cook, covered, for about 2 minutes or until melted. Makes 4 servings.

VARIATION
● PORTOBELLO MUSHROOM SLICES: Slice mushroom caps crosswise into 3/4-inch (2 cm) thick strips. Reduce vinegar to 2 tbsp (25 mL). Reduce cooking time to about 5 minutes, turning once.

TIPS
● Grilled portobello mushrooms paired with grilled sweet pepper on a kaiser roll make delectable sandwiches.
● To make Parmesan shavings, buy Parmigiano Reggiano cheese in a block and use a sharp vegetable peeler to shave the curls straight off the block.

Lamb with Tropical Tastes

1	butterflied leg of lamb (3 lb/1.5 kg)	1
5	green onions, minced	5
4	cloves garlic, minced	4
1/4 cup	orange juice	50 mL
3 tbsp	sodium-reduced soy sauce	50 mL
1 tbsp	vegetable oil	15 mL
2 tsp	ground allspice	10 mL
2 tsp	white vinegar	10 mL
1/2 tsp	each dried thyme, salt and pepper	2 mL
1/2 tsp	hot pepper sauce	2 mL
1/4 tsp	cinnamon	1 mL
	FRUIT SALSA	
1	can (14 oz/398 mL) crushed pineapple	1
2 cups	diced seeded peeled cantaloupe	500 mL
3	green onions, chopped	3
1/2 cup	diced sweet red pepper	125 mL
1 tsp	grated lime rind	5 mL
1 tbsp	lime juice	15 mL
1/4 tsp	hot pepper sauce	1 mL
Pinch	salt	Pinch

● Trim fat from lamb. In large shallow glass dish, combine onions, garlic, orange juice, soy sauce, oil, allspice, vinegar, thyme, salt, pepper, hot pepper sauce and cinnamon; add lamb, turning to coat. Cover and marinate in refrigerator for at least 8 hours or for up to 24 hours, turning occasionally. Let stand at room temperature for 30 minutes.

● FRUIT SALSA: Meanwhile, drain pineapple, reserving 1 tbsp (15 mL) juice. In glass bowl, gently stir together pineapple and reserved juice, cantaloupe, onions, red pepper, lime rind and juice, hot pepper sauce and salt. Cover and let stand for 1 hour.

● Reserving marinade, place lamb on greased grill over medium-high heat; close lid and cook, turning 4 times and basting with marinade once per side, for 20 to 30 minutes or until meat thermometer registers 140°F (60°C) rare, or for 35 to 40 minutes or until 150°F (65°C) for medium-rare.

● Transfer to cutting board and tent with foil; let stand for 10 minutes before carving. Serve with Fruit Salsa. Makes 10 servings.

TIP: If the butterflied leg of lamb is not in one piece or is uneven, skewer together to help cook it evenly.

Conjure up the Caribbean with a leg of lamb marinated with jerk spices and complemented by a zesty fresh fruit salsa.

Per serving: about
- 210 calories
- 8 g fat
- good source of iron
- 24 g protein
- 10 g carbohydrate

Grilled Radicchio

2	heads radicchio	2
1 tbsp	olive oil	15 mL
1/4 tsp	each salt and pepper	1 mL

● Slice radicchio in half lengthwise. Making sure leaves stay attached to core, rinse under running water; pat dry. Brush both sides with oil; sprinkle with salt and pepper.

● Place on greased grill over medium-high heat; close lid and cook, turning once, for 8 to 10 minutes or until core is tender when pierced with fork and leaves are browned. Makes 4 servings.

Grilling mellows the usually bitter radicchio into a surprisingly delicious treat with smoky overtones. Pair it with lamb — chops or a butterflied leg — or a nice juicy beef sirloin.

Per serving: about
- 50 calories
- 4 g fat
- 1 g protein
- 4 g carbohydrate

Spinach-Stuffed Leg of Lamb ◄

1	boneless butterflied leg of lamb (3 lb/1.5 kg)	1
1/2 tsp	pepper	2 mL
1/4 tsp	salt	1 mL
1 tsp	dried oregano	5 mL
3 cups	chicken stock	750 mL
1/4 cup	dry white wine	50 mL
1 tbsp	all-purpose flour	15 mL
	STUFFING	
1	pkg (10 oz/284 g) fresh spinach	1
1 tbsp	butter	15 mL
1	onion, finely chopped	1
2	cloves garlic, minced	2
1 tsp	dried oregano	5 mL
1/2 tsp	pepper	2 mL
1/4 tsp	salt	1 mL
1/2 cup	shredded Asiago or freshly grated Parmesan cheese	125 mL
1/2 cup	fresh bread crumbs	125 mL
1/3 cup	toasted pine nuts	75 mL
1	egg, beaten	1

● STUFFING: Trim and rinse spinach; shake off excess water. In large saucepan, cook spinach, covered and with just the water clinging to leaves, over medium heat for 5 minutes or until wilted. Drain in sieve, pressing out liquid completely. Chop coarsely; place in bowl and set aside. In nonstick skillet, melt butter over medium heat; cook onion, garlic, oregano, pepper and salt, stirring often, for about 5 minutes or until softened. Add to spinach; let cool completely. Add Asiago cheese, bread crumbs, pine nuts and egg, stirring until well combined.

● Trim excess fat from lamb, leaving thin layer; place, fat side down, on work surface. Sprinkle with half each of the pepper and salt. Spread with spinach mixture, leaving 1-inch (2.5 cm) border uncovered. Starting at narrow end, roll up jelly roll-style.

● Fasten each end of roll with poultry pins or skewers; tie at 1-inch (2.5 cm) intervals with kitchen string. Rub with oregano and remaining pepper and salt. Place on greased rack in roasting pan; pour in 1 cup (250 mL) of the chicken stock and wine.

● Roast in 325°F (160°C) oven, basting occasionally and adding more of the stock if necessary to maintain level, for 1-1/2 hours or until meat thermometer registers 140°F (60°C) for rare or 160°F (70°C) for medium.

● Transfer lamb to cutting board and tent with foil; let stand for 15 minutes before removing string and pins and carving into 1/2-inch (1 cm) thick slices.

● Meanwhile, skim fat from roasting pan. Place roasting pan over medium-high heat. Stir flour and 2 tbsp (25 mL) stock into pan drippings; cook, stirring, for 1 minute. Add remaining stock; bring to boil. Reduce heat and simmer, whisking, for 5 minutes or until thickened slightly; strain and serve with lamb. Makes 8 servings.

● STUFFING VARIATION: Add 1 tsp (5 mL) dried basil along with oregano. Replace Asiago with fontina cheese. Add 1/2 cup (125 mL) diced sweet red pepper along with onions.

A boneless leg of lamb with a spinach, oregano, garlic and tangy cheese stuffing is an impressive invitation to a special dinner. It's also simple to make — and a breeze to slice and serve.

Per serving: about
- 295 calories
- 14 g fat
- excellent source of iron
- 37 g protein
- 7 g carbohydrate

TIPS

● To replace wine, substitute chicken stock and add 1 tbsp (15 mL) white wine vinegar.

● Allowing a roast to stand for a few minutes before slicing lets the juices redistribute evenly throughout the meat. Covering the roast with foil, called "tenting," keeps the outside hot.

Really Good Basic Bread ▶

So maybe you're not a bread maker yet. Here's how to get started on the staff of life. Great loaves are guaranteed, either by hand or in the bread machine.

Per slice: about
• 120 calories • 3 g protein
• 2 g fat • 22 g carbohydrate

1 tsp	granulated sugar	5 mL
1 cup	warm water	250 mL
1	pkg active dry yeast (or 1 tbsp/15 mL)	1
1 cup	milk	250 mL
2 tbsp	granulated sugar	25 mL
2 tbsp	butter	25 mL
1 tsp	salt	5 mL
5 cups	(approx) all-purpose flour	1.25 L
1	egg yolk	1
1 tbsp	water	15 mL

● In large bowl, dissolve 1 tsp (5 mL) sugar in warm water. Sprinkle in yeast; let stand for 10 minutes or until frothy.

● Meanwhile, heat together milk, 2 tbsp (25 mL) sugar, butter and salt over low heat until butter is melted; let cool to lukewarm.

● Add milk mixture to yeast mixture. With electric mixer, gradually beat in 3 cups (750 mL) of the flour until smooth. With wooden spoon, gradually stir in enough of the remaining flour to make stiff dough.

● Turn out onto lightly floured surface. Knead for 10 minutes or until smooth and elastic. Place in greased bowl, turning to grease all over. Cover with plastic wrap; let rise in warm spot until doubled in bulk, 1 to 1-1/2 hours.

● Punch down dough; turn out onto lightly floured surface. Knead into ball. Cover with tea towel; let rest for 10 minutes. Divide in half; knead each portion into smooth ball.

● Gently pull each ball into 11- x 8-inch (28 x 20 cm) rectangle. Starting at 1 narrow end, roll up tightly into cylinder; pinch all along seam to smooth and seal. Fit, seam side down, into two greased 8- x 4-inch (1.5 L) loaf pans. Cover and let rise until doubled in bulk, about 1 hour.

● Whisk egg yolk with water; brush over loaves. Bake in 400°F (200°C) oven for about 30 minutes or until golden brown and bottoms sound hollow when tapped. Remove from pans. Let cool on racks. Makes 2 loaves, 12 slices each.

BREAD MACHINE METHOD

In order, place in pan: 1/2 cup (125 mL) each water and milk, 1 tbsp (15 mL) each granulated sugar and cubed butter, 1/2 tsp (2 mL) salt and 3 cups (750 mL) all-purpose flour. Sprinkle 1-1/4 tsp (6 mL) quick-rising active dry yeast over top, making sure yeast does not touch liquid mixture. Choose basic setting or regular/light setting. Let baked loaf cool on rack.

Sweet Endings

Whether it's a dessert for a special occasion or simply the pleasure and challenge of creating a spectacular new take on pastry, chocolate or fruit, the weekends are definitely the time to indulge. Here's our most luscious selection of sweet endings ever!

Mocha Ice Cream Brownie Bombe ▶

How about a dessert for chocolate and coffee lovers alike? A moist chocolate brownie is the base for chocolate and coffee ice cream, with a luscious chocolate sauce swirled over the top.

Per serving: about
- 405 calories
- 28 g fat
- 5 g protein
- 40 g carbohydrate

4 cups	coffee ice cream	1 L
4 cups	chocolate ice cream	1 L
8 oz	bittersweet chocolate, finely chopped	250 g
1 cup	whipping cream	250 mL
	BROWNIE BASE	
1 cup	butter	250 mL
1 cup	sifted unsweetened cocoa powder	250 mL
4	eggs	4
1-1/2 cups	granulated sugar	375 mL
1/4 cup	coffee liqueur or brewed espresso	50 mL
1 tsp	vanilla or rum extract	5 mL
1/2 cup	all-purpose flour	125 mL

● BROWNIE BASE: In small saucepan, melt butter over low heat; stir in cocoa powder until blended. Set aside.

● In bowl, beat eggs with sugar until pale and thickened; stir in liqueur and vanilla. Fold in cocoa mixture, then flour. Pour into greased and floured 9-inch (2.5 L) springform pan; bake in 350°F (180°C) oven for 35 minutes or until set but still slightly jiggly in center. Transfer to rack; let cool for 1 hour. Remove side of pan; let cool completely.

● Let coffee ice cream stand at room temperature for 20 minutes or until softened. Line 9-inch-diameter (2.5 L) bowl with plastic wrap, leaving 3-inch (8 cm) overhang. Line bowl with even layer of coffee ice cream, leaving 1-inch (2.5 cm) space at top. Freeze for about 30 minutes or until firm.

● Fill with chocolate ice cream, pressing down and smoothing top, leaving 1-inch (2.5 cm) space at top. Cover with plastic wrap; freeze for about 2 hours or until firm.

● Place chocolate in bowl. In small saucepan, heat cream just until bubbles form around edge of pan; pour over chocolate, stirring until melted. Let cool.

● Cut off any raised edges from top of brownie base. Spread with 1/4 cup (50 mL) of the chocolate mixture. Remove plastic wrap from frozen ice cream; invert brownie base on top, pressing against ice cream. Cover with plastic wrap; freeze for about 1 hour or until firm.

● Remove plastic wrap. Invert onto serving plate; remove bowl and plastic wrap. Spoon 1/4 cup (50 mL) of the remaining chocolate mixture into piping bag; set aside. Working quickly, spread remaining chocolate mixture over ice cream and brownie. Freeze for about 30 minutes or until firm.

● Pipe chocolate mixture in squiggles all over bombe. Freeze for about 30 minutes or until firm. *(Bombe can be covered loosely with plastic wrap and stored in rigid container in freezer for up to 1 week.)* Let stand at room temperature for 15 minutes before serving. Makes 20 servings.

White Chocolate Mousse with Raspberry Swirl

Puréed raspberries give a fresh, fruity lift to an elegant dessert. Layer the chocolate mousse and raspberry purée in individual parfait glasses, if you like (photo, p. 69).

Per serving: about
- 250 calories
- 19 g fat
- 4 g protein
- 18 g carbohydrate

2 cups	plain yogurt	500 mL
1	pkg (300 g) frozen unsweetened raspberries, thawed	1
1/4 cup	icing sugar	50 mL
12 oz	white chocolate, chopped	375 g
2 cups	whipping cream	500 mL
	Fresh raspberries	
	Mint leaves	

● Place yogurt in cheesecloth-lined strainer set over bowl; drain in refrigerator for at least 6 hours or for up to 12 hours or until reduced to 1 cup (250 mL). Discard liquid.

● In sieve set over measuring cup, drain 1/2 cup (125 mL) juice from raspberries; reserve for another use. Transfer raspberries and remaining juice to food processor or blender; purée with icing sugar using on/off motion. Strain through sieve to remove seeds and make about 1 cup (250 mL) purée. Let purée stand at room temperature for 1 hour.

● In heatproof bowl set over hot (not boiling) water, melt chocolate with 1/2 cup (125 mL) of the cream, without stirring. Remove from heat; whisk until smooth. Let cool to room temperature, stirring occasionally.

● In large bowl, whip remaining cream. In separate bowl, whisk drained yogurt until smooth; fold into whipped cream. Fold one-third of the cream mixture into chocolate mixture, then fold chocolate mixture back into cream mixture.

● Spoon one-third of the chocolate mixture into 10-cup (2.5 L) trifle bowl. Spoon one-third of the raspberry sauce, by tablespoonfuls (15 mL), over top. Using handle of spoon, swirl sauce through chocolate mixture. Repeat twice with remaining chocolate mixture and raspberry sauce. Cover and refrigerate for at least 1 hour or for up to 8 hours.

● To serve, let stand at room temperature for about 30 minutes or until slightly softened. Garnish with fresh raspberries and mint leaves. Makes 12 to 16 servings.

TIP: To use individually quick frozen (IQF) raspberries for garnish, let thaw just until no longer icy. You can use scented geranium leaves for garnish, too.

White Chocolate Fondue

Scrumptious is the only way to describe this white-chocolate update of a sixties favorite!

Per serving: about
- 300 calories
- 22 g fat
- 3 g protein
- 24 g carbohydrate

6 oz	white chocolate, chopped	175 g
1/3 cup	whipping cream	75 mL
2 tbsp	brandy or rum (optional)	25 mL

● In small heavy saucepan with flameproof handle, mix chocolate with cream.

● Place on grill or stove top over low heat; warm, stirring constantly, until chocolate is barely melted. Remove from heat; stir in brandy (if using). Makes 3/4 cup (175 mL), or 4 servings.

TIP: Serve with fresh strawberries (leave on the stems), pineapple chunks, melon spears, banana chunks or even squares of banana bread.

Sherbet Cream Puffs ▼

4 cups	orange sherbet	1 L
	CHOUX PASTRY	
1 cup	water	250 mL
1/2 cup	butter	125 mL
Pinch	salt	Pinch
1-1/2 cups	all-purpose flour	300 mL
4	eggs, beaten	4
	GLAZE	
1	egg	1
1 tbsp	water	15 mL
	CHOCOLATE SAUCE	
3/4 cup	whipping cream	175 mL
6 oz	semisweet chocolate, chopped	175 g

● Line baking sheet with parchment paper, or grease and dust with flour. Trace ten 2-1/2 inch (6 cm) circles, 2 inches (5 cm) apart, on paper; set aside.

● CHOUX PASTRY: In heavy saucepan, bring water, butter and salt just to boil over high heat; remove from heat. Add flour all at once; stir vigorously with wooden spoon until mixture comes away from side of pan in smooth ball.

● Reduce heat to medium-low. Cook mixture, stirring constantly, for 2 minutes or until coating begins to form on bottom of pan. Turn out into large bowl; stir for 30 seconds to cool slightly.

● Make well in center of dough. Using electric mixer, beat in eggs, one quarter at a time, beating well after each addition; beat until smooth, shiny, and choux pastry just holds its shape when lifted.

● Using large pastry bag fitted with 1/2-inch (1 cm) star tip and starting at center, pipe pastry to fill each circle, raising bag while continually piping to form 2 smaller circles on top to resemble beehive. (Or drop by 1/4 cup/50 mL, spreading with spoon to fill circle and shaping to form beehive.)

● GLAZE: Beat egg with water; brush quickly over pastry, making sure none drips onto paper.

● Bake in 425°F (220°C) oven for 20 minutes. Reduce heat to 375°F (190°C); bake for 10 to 15 minutes or until golden and crisp. With sharp knife, pierce small hole in side of each. Bake for 5 minutes. Turn off oven; let cream puffs stand in oven for 10 minutes to dry. Transfer to rack; let cool.

● CHOCOLATE SAUCE: Meanwhile, in heavy saucepan, bring cream to boil. In bowl, pour cream over chocolate, whisking until melted.

● Cut cream puffs in half horizontally. Scoop sherbet into bottom half; replace top. Drizzle with chocolate sauce. Makes 10 servings.

VARIATION

● FROZEN ICE-CREAM PUFFS: Remove moist bits of dough inside cream puffs. Substitute 4 cups (1 L) vanilla, chocolate or raspberry ice cream for the sherbet. Freeze for at least 2 hours or until solid; wrap individually and store in airtight container for up to 1 week. To serve, let stand at room temperature for 5 minutes before drizzling with hot chocolate sauce.

Surprisingly easy to prepare, these puffs can be served year-round with a variety of fillings — ice cream, sorbet, sherbet or whipped cream — plus a fruit, chocolate or caramel sauce.

Per serving: about
- 430 calories
- 26 g fat
- 7 g protein
- 46 g carbohydrate

Pear Strudel

Just imagine layers of flaky, buttery phyllo encasing a fragrant filling of pears with just a hint of lemon and nutmeg. You'll have an impressive dessert on hand with this already waiting in the freezer.

Per serving: about
- 195 calories
- 7 g fat
- 2 g protein
- 33 g carbohydrate

2 tbsp	granulated sugar	25 mL
1/2 tsp	cinnamon	2 mL
6	sheets phyllo pastry	6
1/4 cup	butter, melted	50 mL
1 tbsp	fine dry bread crumbs	15 mL
	Icing sugar	
	FILLING	
1/3 cup	granulated sugar	75 mL
2 tsp	grated lemon rind	10 mL
1 tbsp	lemon juice	15 mL
1/4 tsp	nutmeg	1 mL
Pinch	cinnamon	Pinch
3 cups	chopped peeled pears	750 mL
1 tbsp	cornstarch	15 mL

● FILLING: In saucepan, combine sugar, lemon rind and juice, nutmeg and cinnamon; cook over medium heat, stirring, until sugar is dissolved. Add pears and reduce heat to medium-low. Cover and cook for 3 minutes; uncover and cook, stirring occasionally, for about 3 minutes longer or until pears are tender. Dissolve conrstarch in 2 tbsp (25 mL) cold water; stir into pears and cook, stirring, for 30 seconds or until thickened. Let cool completely.

● In small bowl, combine granulated sugar and cinnamon. Place 1 sheet of phyllo on waxed paper-lined work surface; cover remaining phyllo with damp tea towel to prevent drying out. Lightly brush sheet with some of the butter; sprinkle with about 1 tsp (5 mL) of the sugar mixture.

● Place second phyllo sheet on top; brush with butter and sprinkle with about 1 tsp (5 mL) of the sugar mixture. Repeat layers 3 times, using up all of sugar mixture. Top with last sheet of phyllo; brush with butter and sprinkle with bread crumbs.

● About 2 inches (5 cm) from 1 long edge of pastry, spoon pear mixture lengthwise along pastry in 3-inch (8 cm) wide strip, leaving 2-inch (5 cm) border of pastry at each short end.

● Using waxed paper as guide and starting at long edge nearest filling, carefully roll up phyllo over filling jelly roll-style, folding in edges and allowing a little slack for expansion. Brush with butter. *(Strudel can be prepared to this point, frozen, then wrapped in plastic wrap and foil. Freeze in rigid airtight container for up to 1 month. Unwrap and let stand for 1-1/2 hours before baking.)*

● Carefully place strudel, seam side down, on greased baking sheet. Cut 7 evenly spaced diagonal slits in top. Bake in 400°F (200°C) oven for 30 to 40 minutes or until crisp and golden. Transfer to rack or serving platter. Let cool until warm or at room temperature; dust with icing sugar. Makes 8 servings.

PERFECT PEARS

Ripe, juicy but still-firm pears are a must for pies and strudels. Because pears ripen from the core out and are delicate when fully ripe, they're always picked and sold green, so you have to ripen them yourself.

● Enclose them in a single layer in a paper bag for speedy ripening, or on a tray if there's no hurry, and let ripen at room temperature out of sunlight. Use up immediately when golden and slightly "giving" to the touch, or refrigerate for consumption within a day or two.

Chocolate Chess Pie ▼

	Pastry for 9-inch (23 cm) single-crust pie	
2 oz	unsweetened chocolate, chopped	60 g
1/2 cup	butter, cubed	125 mL
4	eggs	4
1-1/4 cups	granulated sugar	300 mL
2 tbsp	all-purpose flour	25 mL
Pinch	salt	Pinch
2 tbsp	whipping cream	25 mL
1 tbsp	bourbon or rum (optional)	15 mL
1/2 tsp	vanilla	2 mL
	TOPPING	
1/2 cup	whipping cream	125 mL
1 tbsp	bourbon or rum	15 mL
1/2 tsp	granulated sugar	2 mL

● On lightly floured surface, roll out pastry and fit into 9-inch (23 cm) pie plate. Trim, leaving 1-inch (2.5 cm) overhang; fold under and flute edge. Cut out decorative shapes from remaining pastry. Cover and refrigerate for at least 30 minutes or for up to 24 hours.

● Using fork, prick shell all over. Line with foil; fill evenly with pie weights or dried beans. Place pastry cutouts on lightly greased baking sheet. Bake pie shell and pastry cutouts in 400°F (200°C) oven for 15 minutes. Remove foil and weights; bake for 5 minutes. Transfer pie shell and pastry cutouts to rack.

● Meanwhile, in small saucepan, melt chocolate with butter over low heat; set aside. In bowl, beat eggs lightly; whisk in sugar until blended. Whisk in flour and salt. Whisk in chocolate mixture, cream, bourbon (if using) and vanilla, whisking well to combine. Pour into prepared pie shell.

● Bake in 325°F (160°C) oven for about 35 minutes or just until center is set and no longer jiggly and top is slightly crusty. Let cool on rack. *(Pie can be stored at room temperature for up to 6 hours.)* Arrange pastry cutouts on top of pie.

● TOPPING: In bowl, whip together cream, bourbon and sugar. Garnish each serving with dollop of topping. Makes 10 servings.

A *rich and creamy custard filling is tempered with pure chocolate. A small wedge will certainly satisfy guests, but chocolate lovers may clamor for more.*

Per serving: about
- 390 calories
- 5 g protein
- 26 g fat
- 36 g carbohydrate

TIP: If you're short of time, use a frozen pie shell instead of making your own pastry.

Blueberry Pie ▼

A *pat-in crust makes a pie like this a pie that anybody can make. For true blueberry flavor, look for smaller low-bush varieties — fresh in the summer or frozen the rest of the year.*

Per serving: about
- 425 calories
- 5 g protein
- 23 g fat
- 52 g carbohydrate

1-1/4 cups	all-purpose flour	300 mL
3 tbsp	icing sugar	50 mL
Pinch	salt	Pinch
2/3 cup	cold butter, cubed	150 mL
	FILLING	
2/3 cup	granulated sugar	150 mL
3 tbsp	cornstarch	50 mL
Pinch	salt	Pinch
5 cups	blueberries	1.25 L
1/2 tsp	finely grated lemon rind	2 mL
2 tbsp	lemon juice	25 mL
1 tbsp	butter	15 mL
	TOPPING	
1 cup	plain low-fat yogurt	250 mL
1/2 cup	whipping cream	125 mL

● In bowl, stir together flour, sugar and salt. Using pastry blender or two knives, cut in butter until crumbly. Using hands, press mixture into small handfuls until smooth and dough holds together. Press evenly onto bottom and up side of 10-inch (25 cm) flan pan with removable bottom.

● Using fork, prick crust at 1-inch (2.5 cm) intervals. Bake in 350°F (180°C) oven for about 20 minutes or until light sandy color. Let cool on rack.

● FILLING: Meanwhile, in saucepan, stir together sugar, cornstarch and salt. Whisk in 1/3 cup (75 mL) cold water, 2 cups (500 mL) of the blueberries and lemon rind. Bring to simmer over medium heat; reduce heat and simmer gently, stirring often, for about 10 minutes or until glossy and thickened. Remove from heat. Stir in lemon juice and butter. Let cool slightly.

● Gently stir remaining berries into saucepan. Spoon into prepared crust, smoothing top. Refrigerate for about 30 minutes or until set. *(Pie can be prepared to this point and refrigerated for up to 8 hours.)*

● TOPPING: Spoon yogurt into cheesecloth-lined sieve set over bowl. Let drain in refrigerator for 4 hours or until reduced to 3/4 cup (175 mL). Discard liquid. In bowl, whip cream; stir one-quarter into yogurt. Fold in remaining cream. Spoon over pie. Makes 8 servings.

Ricotta Cheesecake with Citrus Compote

1 cup	graham cracker crumbs	250 mL
2 tbsp	butter, melted	25 mL
	FILLING	
12 oz	ricotta cheese	375 g
8 oz	light cream cheese, softened	250 g
1/2 cup	granulated sugar	125 mL
2	eggs	2
1/2 cup	light sour cream	125 mL
2 tbsp	all-purpose flour	25 mL
2 tsp	vanilla	10 mL
1-1/2 tsp	finely grated orange rind	7 mL
	CITRUS COMPOTE	
2	each oranges and pink grapefruit	2
1/2 tsp	cornstarch	2 mL

● In bowl, stir graham cracker crumbs with butter until moistened; press evenly onto bottom of greased 8-inch (2 L) springform pan. Center pan on square of foil; press foil up to cover side of pan. Bake in 350°F (180°C) oven for 8 minutes or until firm. Let cool.

● FILLING: In food processor, purée together ricotta, cream cheese and sugar until smooth. Blend in eggs, one at a time. Blend in sour cream, flour, vanilla and orange rind. Pour over baked crust.

● Set foil-wrapped pan in larger pan; pour in enough hot water to come 1 inch (2.5 cm) up sides. Bake in 325°F (160°C) oven for 50 to 60 minutes or until set. Remove from water. Run knife around edge of cake; remove foil and let cool on rack. Cover and refrigerate for 8 hours. *(Cheesecake can be prepared to this point; covered and stored in refrigerator for up to 2 days.)* Remove side of pan.

● CITRUS COMPOTE: Using knife and working over bowl to catch juices, cut peel and white pith from oranges and grapefruit; cut between membrane to remove segments, adding segments to bowl. Let stand for 10 minutes.

● Drain juices into small saucepan; stir in cornstarch. Bring to boil over medium heat; cook, stirring, for about 3 minutes or until thickened. Stir back into fruit mixture; let stand until cooled to room temperature before serving with cheesecake. Makes 8 servings.

Cheesecakes made with full-fat cream cheese are, naturally, high in fat. Here is a lighter version with ricotta and just enough light cream cheese and sour cream for a smooth, satisfying taste.

Per serving: about
- 360 calories
- 12 g protein
- 19 g fat
- 37 g carbohydrate
- good source of calcium

TIP: If cheesecake is exposed to sudden temperature change when baking, or bakes in too hot an oven for too long, cracks may appear as the cheesecake cools. Resist opening the oven door. Be sure to bake the cake in a water bath; this ensures even, slow, moist cooking.

PERFECT PASTRY

In bowl, mix 3 cups (750 mL) all-purpose flour with 1 tsp (5 mL) salt; cut in 1/2 cup (125 mL) each butter and lard or shortening. Beat together 1 egg, 2 tsp (10 mL) vinegar and enough ice water to make 2/3 cup (150 mL); sprinkle over top and toss until dough holds together. Press into 2 discs. Makes enough for 2 single-crust pies or 1 double-crust 9-inch (23 cm) pie. *(Pastry can be wrapped well in plastic wrap and frozen for up to 1 month.)*

Raspberry Mirror Cheesecake ▶

*C*elebrate any occasion *with this elegant-looking, exquisite-tasting cheesecake!*

Per serving: about
• 340 g calories   • 5 g protein
• 22 g fat   • 34 g carbohydrate

TIP: A few fresh raspberries, fresh mint leaves and rose petals make an attractive garnish.

1-1/4 cups	chocolate wafer cookie crumbs	300 mL
1/3 cup	butter, melted	75 mL
	FILLING	
8 oz	semisweet chocolate, coarsely chopped	250 g
2	pkg (250 g each) cream cheese, softened	2
1 cup	granulated sugar	250 mL
3	eggs	3
1 tsp	vanilla	5 mL
	GLAZE	
1	pkg (300 g) frozen raspberries, thawed	1
1/2 cup	granulated sugar	125 mL
1-1/2 tsp	gelatin	7 mL

● Assemble 9-inch (2.5 L) springform pan with base lip-side down. Stir cookie crumbs with butter until moistened; with back of spoon, press evenly onto bottom of pan. Center pan on large wide piece of foil; press foil up to cover side of pan. Bake in 325°F (160°C) oven for 5 minutes. Set aside.

● FILLING: Meanwhile, in large heatproof bowl set over hot (not boiling) water, melt chocolate; stir until smooth. Let cool to room temperature.

● In separate bowl, beat cream cheese with sugar for 2 minutes or until smooth and light. Beat in eggs, one at a time. Beat in vanilla. Stir half into cooled chocolate; scrape onto baked crust. Gently pour remaining cream cheese mixture evenly over top.

● Set foil-wrapped pan in larger pan; pour in enough hot water to come 1 inch (2.5 cm) up sides. Bake in 325°F (160°C) oven for 1 hour or just until no longer shiny and top does not jiggle. Turn oven off. Let cool in oven for 1 hour. Remove from oven and water; let cool on rack to room temperature. Refrigerate, uncovered, until chilled. *(Cheesecake can be prepared to this point, covered and stored in refrigerator for up to 2 days.)*

● GLAZE: Meanwhile, press raspberries through fine sieve to make 3/4 cup (175 mL) juice. In saucepan, bring juice and sugar to boil over medium-high heat; cook, stirring, for 30 seconds or until sugar is dissolved.

● In bowl, whisk together 1/4 cup (50 mL) of the glaze and gelatin; let stand for 1 minute. Stir in remaining raspberry mixture; refrigerate, stirring often, for about 1 hour or until consistency of liquid honey. Pour over chilled cake, gently spreading with back of spoon to cover top evenly. Refrigerate for 1 hour or until glaze is set. Makes 16 servings.

MAKING DESSERTS LOOK GLAMOROUS

● To make the lime curl garnish in the photo of the Lime Custard with Mango, a few hours before serving, use a cannel knife or paring knife to cut a continuous narrow strip of peel for each serving. Curl firmly around the handle of a wooden spoon; wrap curl with damp towels and chill. To serve, uncurl over custard.

● To make the spider web design in the Crème Anglaise (p. 80), drizzle chocolate sauce in circle in crème anglaise. Space 8 dots of chocolate sauce around the circle and place 1 in center of circle. Pull tip of pointed knife from circle toward each dot to create web, and then pull knife through dots outside circle to form hearts. Pull knife through center dot to echo lines radiating from web. The best way to drizzle sauce evenly is to use a ketchup-type plastic squeeze bottle you've reserved exclusively for decorating.

Chocolate Layer Cake ◄

3/4 cup	unsalted butter, softened	175 mL
1-1/2 cups	granulated sugar	375 mL
7	eggs, separated	7
1-1/2 tsp	vanilla	7 mL
1-1/2 cups	sifted cake-and-pastry flour	375 mL
2/3 cup	unsweetened cocoa powder	150 mL
1-1/2 tsp	baking soda	7 mL
3/4 cup	buttermilk	175 mL

CHOCOLATE ICING		
1-1/2 cups	unsalted butter, softened	375 mL
1/2 cup	whipping cream	125 mL
1 tbsp	vanilla	15 mL
3 cups	icing sugar	750 mL
6 oz	unsweetened chocolate, melted and cooled	175 g

● Grease three 9-inch (1.5 L) round cake pans. Cut three 9-inch (23 cm) rounds of parchment or waxed paper; place in pans, then turn greased side up.

● In bowl, with electric beaters, beat butter with 3/4 cup (175 mL) of the sugar until fluffy. Beat in egg yolks, one at a time, beating well after each addition. Beat in vanilla.

● Sift together flour, cocoa and baking soda. Using wooden spoon, stir into butter mixture alternately with buttermilk, making 3 additions of flour mixture and 2 of buttermilk.

● In separate bowl and using clean beaters, beat egg whites until soft peaks form; gradually beat in remaining sugar until stiff peaks form. With spatula, fold one-quarter into batter; fold in remaining egg whites in 2 additions. Divide among pans, smoothing tops.

● Bake in center of 350°F (180°C) oven for 25 to 30 minutes or until cake tester inserted in center comes out clean and top springs back when lightly touched. Let cool in pans on rack for 30 minutes. Remove from pans; let cool completely, paper side down, on rack.

● CHOCOLATE ICING: In bowl, and using electric beaters, beat butter until fluffy; gradually beat in cream. Beat in vanilla, icing sugar, 1 cup (250 mL) at a time. Beat in melted chocolate until fluffy and smooth.

● Peel paper from bottom of cake layers; place one layer on cake plate; spread 1 cup (250 mL) icing over top. Repeat with next layer. Place third layer on top. Spread remaining icing over top and side of cake. Makes 16 servings.

VARIATION

● MOCHA FUDGE CAKE: For icing, dissolve 2 tbsp (25 mL) instant espresso powder or instant coffee granules in vanilla.

There's no better sweet ending to a special family dinner than this classic chocolate cake featuring three light-as-a-feather chocolate layers with thick, creamy filling and icing. Memories will definitely be made of this!

Per serving: about
- 545 calories
- 38 g fat
- good source of iron
- 6 g protein
- 52 g carbohydrate

TIP: Before icing, layers can be wrapped in plastic wrap and refrigerated for up to 1 day, or overwrapped in foil and frozen in rigid airtight container for up to 2 months.

Tattingstone Inn Chocolate Pâté ▲

Wolfville, Nova Scotia, is a gourmet traveler's paradise. Among the excellent inns and restaurants is the historic, elegantly furnished Tattingstone Inn. Their luscious chocolate pâté keeps local residents and visitors alike coming back for more.

Per serving: about
- 575 calories
- 48 g fat
- good source of iron
- 6 g protein
- 39 g carbohydrate

10 oz	high-quality bittersweet chocolate, chopped	300 g
1 cup	whipping cream	250 mL
2 cups	fresh raspberries	500 mL
	CRÈME ANGLAISE	
4	egg yolks	4
2/3 cup	granulated sugar	150 mL
2 cups	whipping cream	500 mL

● In heatproof bowl set over hot (not boiling) water, stir chocolate with cream until melted. Place plastic wrap directly on surface; refrigerate for at least 8 hours or until firm. *(Pâté can be refrigerated for up to 6 days.)*

● CRÈME ANGLAISE: Meanwhile, in separate heatproof bowl, whisk egg yolks with sugar until light yellow. In saucepan, heat cream over low heat until bubbles form around edge of pan; whisk into yolk mixture.

● Set bowl over simmering water; cook, stirring with wooden spoon, for 5 to 10 minutes or until thick enough to coat back of spoon. Strain through fine sieve into bowl. Place plastic wrap directly on surface; refrigerate until chilled or for up to 3 days.

● To serve, spoon about 1/4 cup (50 mL) Crème Anglaise onto serving plates. Top with small scoop of pâté. Garnish with raspberries. Makes 8 servings.

Sour Cream Fudge Cake

1/2 cup	butter, softened	125 mL
2-1/4 cups	packed brown sugar	550 mL
3	eggs	3
3 oz	unsweetened chocolate, melted and cooled	90 g
1-1/2 tsp	vanilla	7 mL
2-1/2 cups	sifted cake-and-pastry flour	625 mL
2 tsp	baking soda	10 mL
1/4 tsp	salt	1 mL
1 cup	sour cream	250 mL
1 cup	boiling water	250 mL
	ICING	
5 oz	unsweetened chocolate, chopped	150 g
1/3 cup	butter, softened	75 mL
3 cups	icing sugar	750 mL
3/4 cup	milk	175 mL

● In bowl, beat butter until creamy. Gradually beat in sugar; beat for about 5 minutes or until fluffy. Beat in eggs, one at a time. Beat in chocolate and vanilla.

● Stir together flour, baking soda and salt; add to chocolate mixture alternately with sour cream, making 3 additions of dry mixture and 2 of sour cream. Stir in water.

● Divide batter between 2 greased and floured 9-inch (1.5 L) round cake pans. Bake in center of 350°F (180°C) oven for 35 to 40 minutes or until cake tester inserted in center comes out clean and top springs back when touched. Let cool in pans on rack for 30 minutes. Remove from pans; let cool completely.

● ICING: In heatproof bowl set over hot (not boiling) water, melt chocolate. Let cool to room temperature. In separate bowl, beat butter. Gradually beat in chocolate. Beat in sugar alternately with milk until fluffy, making 4 additions of sugar and 3 of milk.

● Place one cake layer on cake plate. Spread 1 cup (250 mL) icing over top. Place other layer on top. Spread remaining icing over top and side. *(Cake can be covered and refrigerated for up to 1 day.)* Makes 16 servings.

Basic, and basically fabulous, this moist chocolatey cake is the perfect ending to any relaxing gathering — especially since it can be assembled a day ahead and refrigerated.

Per serving: about
- 455 calories
- 21 g fat
- good source of iron
- 5 g protein
- 68 g carbohydrate

CHOCOLATE BASICS

The quality of your chocolate dessert depends on the quality of the chocolate. It's worth searching out better brands for the extra-good chocolate taste they provide.
● There is a choice of unsweetened, bittersweet, semisweet, sweet, milk and white chocolate. The most intense chocolate flavor is found in the unsweetened, and diminishes with the sugar found in the other chocolate and the milk products added to milk chocolate and white chocolate. Do not confuse bittersweet chocolate — which is basically interchangeable with semisweet — with the unsweetened, which is pure chocolate liquor, the flavorful component of chocolate.

● Store chocolate in a cool spot for up to 4 months. Avoid storing in the refrigerator or freezer because condensation will form on the surface as it cools and cause chocolate to lump and seize if melted. Chocolate stored in warm conditions may develop a harmless pale covering called "bloom," which will disappear during melting.

● To melt chocolate: Chop first to speed the process. Place in clean dry heatproof bowl or on top of double boiler and set over hot, not boiling, water. Stir as the chocolate melts, taking it off the heat when about three-quarters has melted. There's enough residual heat to melt the remainder; stir occasionally.

Apricot Raspberry Parfait ▲

Who will ever guess that a
dessert this creamy can also
be this low in fat? Thanks to
low-fat yogurt, it's possible —
and positively delicious!

Per serving: about
- 170 calories
- 6 g protein
- 2 g fat
- 34 g carbohydrate
- good source
  of beta-carotene

1	can (14 oz/398 mL) apricots	1
1/4 cup	granulated sugar	50 mL
1	pkg (7 g) unflavored gelatin	1
2 tbsp	lemon juice	25 mL
1/4 tsp	almond extract	1 mL
1 cup	low-fat plain yogurt	250 mL
1	pkg (300 g) frozen unsweetened raspberries, thawed	1

● Drain apricots, reserving 1/4 cup (50 mL) juice; set apricots aside.

● In saucepan or microwaveable dish, combine juice with 3 tbsp (45 mL) of the sugar. Sprinkle gelatin over top; let stand for 5 minutes. Cook over low heat, or microwave at Medium (50% power) for 40 seconds, or until gelatin is dissolved.

● In food processor or blender, purée apricots. Add gelatin mixture, lemon juice and almond extract; purée until smooth. Stir in yogurt. Set aside.

● Press raspberries and juice through sieve into bowl; stir in remaining sugar. Reserve 1/4 cup (50 mL) of the purée for garnish.

● Stir remaining raspberry purée into apricot mixture. Spoon into four parfait or stemmed glasses. Cover and refrigerate for 1-1/2 hours or until set. Spoon reserved raspberry purée over top. *(Parfaits can be refrigerated for up to 2 days.)* Makes 4 servings.

Cranberry Orange Flan

1-1/2 cups	fresh or frozen cranberries	375 mL
1/4 cup	granulated sugar	50 mL
1	strip (2 inches/5 cm long) orange rind	1
1/4 cup	orange juice	50 mL
2 tbsp	orange liqueur (optional)	25 mL

PASTRY CREAM		
1-3/4 cups	milk	425 mL
3	egg yolks	3
1/3 cup	granulated sugar	75 mL
1/3 cup	all-purpose flour	75 mL
2 tsp	butter	10 mL
2 tsp	vanilla	10 mL

PASTRY		
1-1/2 cups	all-purpose flour	375 mL
1 tbsp	granulated sugar	15 mL
1/2 tsp	salt	2 mL
3/4 cup	cold butter, cubed	175 mL

● In saucepan, combine cranberries, sugar, orange rind and juice, and liqueur (if using); bring to boil. Reduce heat to simmer; cook, stirring, for about 10 minutes or until cranberries have popped and sauce is thickened. Strain through sieve into bowl to remove seeds and skins. Cover with plastic wrap; refrigerate until cooled. *(Sauce can be refrigerated for up to 3 days.)*

● PASTRY CREAM: In small saucepan, heat milk over medium heat just until bubbles form around edge. In bowl, whisk egg yolks with sugar; gradually whisk in flour. In thin steady stream, gradually whisk in hot milk.

● Wipe out saucepan and return mixture to pan; cook, whisking constantly, just until beginning to boil. Boil, whisking constantly, for 1 minute or until thickened. Strain through sieve into bowl. Stir in butter and vanilla. Place plastic wrap directly on surface and refrigerate until completely cooled. *(Pastry cream can be refrigerated for up to 3 days.)*

● PASTRY: In large bowl, combine flour, sugar and salt. Using pastry blender or two knives, cut in butter until mixture resembles fine crumbs. Using hands, press mixture into small handfuls until dough holds together; press onto bottom of 10-inch (25 cm) round flan pan with removable bottom.

● Using fork, prick pastry shell all over. Line with foil; fill evenly with pie weights or dried beans. Bake in 375°F (190°C) oven for 20 minutes. Remove foil and weights; bake for 10 minutes or just until golden brown. Transfer to rack; let cool completely. *(Pastry shell can be covered and stored at room temperature for up to 1 day.)*

● Fill pastry shell with pastry cream. Stir cranberry sauce until smooth; spoon over cream, then spread carefully to cover completely. *(Flan can be covered and refrigerated for up to 8 hours.)* Just before serving, remove side of pan. Makes 10 servings.

Here's a showstopper at any buffet table — flaky pat-in pastry with a smooth cream filling and a ruby-red sauce. Garnish with orange slices and sprigs of fresh mint.

Per serving: about
● 315 calories ● 5 g protein
● 17 g fat ● 35 g carbohydrate

Lime Custard with Mango ◄

2-1/2 cups	whipping cream	625 mL
2 tsp	grated lime rind	10 mL
6	egg yolks	6
3 tbsp	granulated sugar	50 mL
1	large mango	1
2 tbsp	passion fruit liqueur or coconut liqueur	25 mL
1 tsp	lime juice	5 mL

● In small saucepan, heat cream and lime rind over medium-high heat just until bubbles form around edge of pan, about 4 minutes; let cool to room temperature.

● In large bowl, whisk egg yolks with sugar until sugar is dissolved, scraping down side of bowl. Pour cream mixture through strainer into egg mixture.

● Place 6 ramekins or 3/4-cup (175 mL) custard cups in 13- x 9-inch (3 L) baking dish. Pour custard evenly into ramekins. Pour enough hot water into baking dish to come halfway up sides of ramekins. Cover tightly and bake in 350°F (180°C) oven for 50 minutes or until knife inserted at edge comes out clean.

● Uncover ramekins; let cool in water bath to room temperature. Remove from water and place on tray; cover and refrigerate for 1 day or until properly set and thoroughly chilled. *(Custards can be refrigerated for up to 2 days.)*

● About 1 hour before serving, remove custards from refrigerator; set aside. Peel and dice mango; place in bowl. Gently stir in liqueur and lime juice; cover and set aside. To serve, spoon fruit evenly over custards and serve immediately. Makes 6 servings.

As smooth as a tropical breeze, this creamy custard profits from a day in the refrigerator to mellow the lime flavor. If you want to omit the liqueur, substitute 2 tbsp (25 mL) lime juice and omit the 1 tsp (5 mL) lime juice in recipe.

Per serving: about
● 460 calories
● 40 g fat
● 5 g protein
● 19 g carbohydrate

Pear Pandowdy

8 cups	chopped peeled pears	2 L
1/3 cup	liquid honey	75 mL
2 tsp	grated lemon rind	10 mL
2 tbsp	lemon juice	25 mL
2 tsp	cornstarch	10 mL
1/2 tsp	nutmeg	2 mL
	TOPPING	
3/4 cup	all-purpose flour	175 mL
1 tbsp	granulated sugar	15 mL
1/2 tsp	grated lemon rind	2 mL
Pinch	salt	Pinch
1/3 cup	cold butter, cubed	75 mL
2 tbsp	lemon juice	25 mL
	GLAZE	
2 tsp	milk	10 mL
1 tsp	granulated sugar	5 mL

● In bowl, toss together pears, honey, lemon rind and juice, cornstarch and nutmeg. Spread in 8-inch (2 L) square baking dish; set aside.

● TOPPING: In bowl, stir together flour, sugar, lemon rind and salt. With pastry blender or two knives, cut in butter until crumbly. Combine 2 tbsp (25 mL) cold water with lemon juice; drizzle over flour mixture, stirring with fork until dough holds together when pressed. Transfer to lightly floured surface; roll out slightly larger than baking dish. Place over fruit, tucking pastry down inside edge of dish.

● GLAZE: Brush pastry with milk; sprinkle with sugar. Cut "X" in center. Bake in 400°F (200°C) oven for 50 minutes or until filling is tender and bubbly and topping is golden. Using sharp knife, cut pastry topping into 2-inch (5 cm) squares, pressing sides of squares down into fruit. Bake for 10 minutes or until golden brown. Makes 8 servings.

A pandowdy is a juicy fruit pudding with a crusty covering. Breaking up the pastry topping and pushing it down into the fruit is called "dowdying."

Per serving: about
● 265 calories
● 9 g fat
● 2 g protein
● 49 g carbohydrate

Upside-Down Pear Gingerbread

For brunch, morning coffee or afternoon tea, here's a mellow gingery upside-down cake to take pleasure in.

Per serving: about
- 315 calories
- 10 g fat
- 4 g protein
- 54 g carbohydrate

2 tbsp	butter, melted	25 mL
1/2 cup	packed brown sugar	125 mL
2	pears (Barlett or Bosc), peeled and sliced	2
	CAKE	
1	egg	1
1/2 cup	granulated sugar	125 mL
1/2 cup	buttermilk	125 mL
1/4 cup	butter, melted	50 mL
1/4 cup	fancy molasses	50 mL
1-1/4 cups	all-purpose flour	300 mL
2 tsp	ginger	10 mL
1 tsp	cinnamon	5 mL
3/4 tsp	baking soda	4 mL
Pinch	each nutmeg and cloves	Pinch

● Spread butter in 8-inch (1.2 L) round cake pan; sprinkle with sugar. Arrange pears, overlapping, in circle to cover pan.

● CAKE: In bowl, beat together egg, sugar, buttermilk, butter and molasses. Stir together flour, ginger, cinnamon, baking soda, nutmeg and cloves; sprinkle into buttermilk mixture, stirring just until moistened. Pour over pears.

● Bake in 375°F (190°C) oven for 50 to 55 minutes or until tester inserted in center comes out clean. Let cool on rack for 15 minutes; invert onto cake plate. Makes 8 servings.

Bumbleberry Cobbler

A homey dessert goes special-occasion and celebrates berries at their very best. The availability of unsweetened frozen fruit is an invitation to make this bubbly cobbler any time of the year. Strawberries can replace half of the blueberries.

Per each of 8 servings: about
- 330 calories
- 17 g fat
- high source of fiber
- 3 g protein
- 44 g carbohydrate

2 cups	blueberries	500 mL
2 cups	raspberries	500 mL
1 cup	blackberries	250 mL
1 cup	chopped apple or pear	250 mL
1/3 cup	granulated sugar	75 mL
2 tbsp	all-purpose flour	25 mL
	TOPPING	
1-1/2 cups	sifted cake-and-pastry flour	375 mL
2 tbsp	granulated sugar	25 mL
2 tsp	baking powder	10 mL
Pinch	salt	Pinch
1/3 cup	butter, cubed	75 mL
3/4 cup	whipping cream	175 mL
	GLAZE	
1 tbsp	whipping cream	15 mL
2 tsp	granulated sugar	10 mL

● In bowl, combine blueberries, raspberries, blackberries and apple. Sprinkle with sugar and flour; toss to coat. Spoon into 8-inch (2 L) square baking dish, leveling top. Set aside.

● TOPPING: In separate bowl, stir together flour, sugar, baking powder and salt. Using pastry blender or two knives, cut in butter until crumbly. Pour in cream, tossing with fork to form soft dough. Turn out onto lightly floured surface; roll out into 1/2-inch thickness. With 2-inch (5 cm) round cookie cutter, cut out circles, rerolling scraps. Arrange over fruit.

● GLAZE: Brush rounds with cream; sprinkle with sugar. Bake in 400°F (200°C) oven for about 30 minutes or until filling is tender and bubbly and topping golden brown and firm underneath. Makes 6 to 8 servings.

Peach Cake Pudding ▼

8 cups	thickly sliced peeled peaches	2 L
2 tbsp	granulated sugar	25 mL
2 tbsp	orange juice	25 mL
1/2 tsp	nutmeg	2 mL
	TOPPING	
1/2 cup	butter, softened	125 mL
1/2 cup	granulated sugar	125 mL
2	eggs	2
1 tsp	grated orange rind	5 mL
1 tsp	vanilla	5 mL
2/3 cup	all-purpose flour	150 mL
1 tsp	baking powder	5 mL
Pinch	salt	Pinch
1/3 cup	milk	75 mL

● In bowl, stir together peaches, sugar, orange juice and nutmeg. Spoon into 11- x 7-inch (2 L) baking dish.

● TOPPING: In bowl, beat butter with sugar until fluffy. Beat in eggs, one at a time. Stir in orange rind and vanilla.

● Combine flour, baking powder and salt; stir half into butter mixture. Stir in milk, then remaining flour mixture. Spread over fruit.

● Bake in 375°F (190°C) oven for 50 minutes or until tester inserted in center of topping comes out clean. Makes 8 servings.

A *cakelike batter folds down over a layer of summer peaches or nectarines and bakes into a blissful treat.*

Per serving: about
- 300 calories
- 13 g fat
- 4 g protein
- 44 g carbohydrate

TIP: If using frozen peaches, be sure to thaw completely and drain off excess juices before using.

Tarte Tatin

Here's a glorious way to enjoy apples — thick wedges of fruit in a warm upside-down pie, oozing with carmelized juices.

Per serving: about
- 365 calories
- 2 g protein
- 8 g fat
- 51 g carbohydrate

1 cup	all-purpose flour	250 mL
1 tbsp	granulated sugar	15 mL
1/4 tsp	salt	1 mL
1/2 cup	unsalted butter, cubed	125 mL
1 tsp	white vinegar	5 mL

	FILLING	
8	Northern Spy apples (about 4 lb/2 kg)	8
2 tbsp	lemon juice	25 mL
1/4 cup	unsalted butter	50 mL
3/4 cup	granulated sugar	175 mL

● In large bowl, combine flour, sugar and salt. Using pastry blender or two knives, cut in butter until in coarse crumbs. In measuring cup, stir vinegar with enough ice water to make 1/4 cup (50 mL). Drizzle over flour mixture, stirring with fork until dough holds together when pressed and adding a few more drops of water if necessary. Press into ball; flatten into disc. Wrap in plastic wrap and refrigerate for at least 30 minutes or for up to 3 days.

● FILLING: Meanwhile, peel, quarter and core apples; cut in half lengthwise. In bowl, toss apples with lemon juice.

● In 8-inch (20 cm) cast-iron skillet, melt butter over medium-high heat. Add sugar; cook, stirring, for 3 to 5 minutes or until starting to bubble. Remove from heat.

● Discarding juice, arrange layer of apples, flat side down, in concentric circles in syrup in pan. Layer remaining apples over top to cover first layer evenly. Cook over medium heat, basting with bubbling syrup, for about 15 minutes or until apples begin to soften and syrup starts to thicken. Cover and cook for 5 minutes or until apples in top layer are just tender. Remove from heat; let cool for 5 minutes.

● Meanwhile, on lightly floured surface, roll out dough to 10-inch (25 cm) circle; cut 4 small steam vents at center. Loosely roll pastry around rolling pin; unroll over apples. Trim pastry and press edge down between apples and pan. Bake in 425°F (220°C) for about 25 minutes or until pastry is golden brown. Let stand for 4 minutes.

● Invert heatproof serving plate over pastry. Wearing oven mitts, grasp plate and pan; invert onto plate. With tongs, quickly arrange apples stuck in pan over top. Serve warm. Makes 8 servings.

TIPS
- ● If Northern Spy apples are unavilable, use 10 Golden Delicious ones, cutting each half into thirds.
- ● Use oven mitts when working with caramelized sugar; it gets extremely hot.
- ● A pastry cloth and stockinette-covered rolling pin make pastry rolling foolproof.

The Contributors

For your easy reference, we have included an alphabetical listing of recipes by contributor.

*In the Canadian Living Test Kitchen. From left: Kate Gammal,
Susan Van Hezewijk, Donna Bartolini (Test Kitchen manager),
Jennifer MacKenzie, Daphna Rabinovitch (associate food editor)
and Elizabeth Baird (food director).*

Photography Credits

DOUGLAS BRADSHAW:
Pages 6, 9, 22, 37, 61, 67,
    71, 78, 87

CLIVE CHAMPION:
front cover

ANDRÉ GALLANT:
Page 80

PAT LACROIX:
Pages 20-21, 38, 84

MICHAEL MAHOVLICH:
Page 60

MICHAEL WARING:
Pages 28, 48, 74

ROBERT WIGINGTON:
Pages 10, 13, 16, 25, 26, 30,
    40, 43, 45, 47, 51, 53,
    54, 57, 58, 64, 69, 73,
    76, 82

Index

Special Thanks

We at *Canadian Living* appreciate the continuing commitment to *Canadian Living's Best* series by Random House of Canada, and particularly the enthusiastic support of president and publisher David Kent and mass marketing sales manager (Ballantine Books) Duncan Shields.

Our magazine and cookbook motto is "Tested Till Perfect" and for that, a vote of thanks to Daphna Rabinovitch, who is also our associate food editor, and to the Test Kitchen staff — Kate Gammal, Heather Howe, Jennifer MacKenzie and Susan Van Hezewijk — under recently appointed manager Donna Bartolini. Thanks also to our food writers, including Margaret Fraser, Carol Ferguson, Anne Lindsay, Jan Main, Dana McCauley, Beth Moffatt, Rose Murray, Iris Raven and Bonnie Stern.

On the editorial side, we are indebted to *Canadian Living*'s senior editors Beverley Renahan, Julia Armstrong and, until recently, Donna Paris, who make sure all recipes are consistent in style and easy to understand — and to Madison Press editors Wanda Nowakowska and Beverley Sotolov for seeing this project through all its editorial stages. Thanks also to Olga Goncalves and Tina Gaudino for their invaluable help behind the scenes.

For the beautiful style and appealing photographs featured in every *Canadian Living's Best* cookbook, our thanks to former creative directors Martha Weaver and Deborah Fadden and to food photographers Fred Bird, Douglas Bradshaw, Clive Champion, Vincent Noguchi, Michael Mahovlich, Michael Waring and Robert Wigington. Food and props stylists also contribute enormously to the appetizing results, and we gratefully acknowledge food stylists Kate Bush, Ruth Gangbar, Jennifer McLagan, Claire Stancer and Olga Truchan, and prop stylists Maggi Jones, Patty LaCroix, Shelly Vlahantones and Janet Walkinshaw. We are also indebted to designer Gord Sibley and his assistant, Dale Vokey, for the wonderful design of the series.

Appreciation is in order for our editor-in-chief, Bonnie Cowan, and our publisher, Caren King, who stand behind the whole food department's vision and passion for great Canadian food.

Elizabeth Baird